Communications
in Computer and Information Science   1775

T0172208

Rationale

The CCIS series is devoted to the publication of proceedings of computer science conferences. Its aim is to efficiently disseminate original research results in informatics in printed and electronic form. While the focus is on publication of peer-reviewed full papers presenting mature work, inclusion of reviewed short papers reporting on work in progress is welcome, too. Besides globally relevant meetings with internationally representative program committees guaranteeing a strict peer-reviewing and paper selection process, conferences run by societies or of high regional or national relevance are also considered for publication.

Topics

The topical scope of CCIS spans the entire spectrum of informatics ranging from foundational topics in the theory of computing to information and communications science and technology and a broad variety of interdisciplinary application fields.

Information for Volume Editors and Authors

Publication in CCIS is free of charge. No royalties are paid, however, we offer registered conference participants temporary free access to the online version of the conference proceedings on SpringerLink (http://link.springer.com) by means of an http referrer from the conference website and/or a number of complimentary printed copies, as specified in the official acceptance email of the event.

CCIS proceedings can be published in time for distribution at conferences or as post-proceedings, and delivered in the form of printed books and/or electronically as USBs and/or e-content licenses for accessing proceedings at SpringerLink. Furthermore, CCIS proceedings are included in the CCIS electronic book series hosted in the SpringerLink digital library at http://link.springer.com/bookseries/7899. Conferences publishing in CCIS are allowed to use Online Conference Service (OCS) for managing the whole proceedings lifecycle (from submission and reviewing to preparing for publication) free of charge.

Publication process

The language of publication is exclusively English. Authors publishing in CCIS have to sign the Springer CCIS copyright transfer form, however, they are free to use their material published in CCIS for substantially changed, more elaborate subsequent publications elsewhere. For the preparation of the camera-ready papers/files, authors have to strictly adhere to the Springer CCIS Authors' Instructions and are strongly encouraged to use the CCIS LaTeX style files or templates.

Abstracting/Indexing

CCIS is abstracted/indexed in DBLP, Google Scholar, EI-Compendex, Mathematical Reviews, SCImago, Scopus. CCIS volumes are also submitted for the inclusion in ISI Proceedings.

How to start

To start the evaluation of your proposal for inclusion in the CCIS series, please send an e-mail to ccis@springer.com.

Vanessa Agredo-Delgado · Pablo H. Ruiz ·
Alexandra Ruiz Gaona ·
María Lili Villegas Ramírez ·
William Joseph Giraldo Orozco
Editors

Advances in Computing

16th Colombian Congress, CCC 2022
Armenia, Colombia, October 17–21, 2022
Revised Selected Papers

 Springer

Editors
Vanessa Agredo-Delgado (iD)
Universidad del Cauca
Popayán, Colombia

Corporación Universitaria Comfacauca
Unicomfacauca
Popayán, Colombia

Alexandra Ruiz Gaona (iD)
University of Quindío
Armenia, Colombia

William Joseph Giraldo Orozco (iD)
University of Quindío
Armenia, Colombia

Pablo H. Ruiz (iD)
Universidad del Cauca
Popayán, Colombia

Corporación Universitaria Comfacauca
Unicomfacauca
Popayán, Colombia

María Lili Villegas Ramírez (iD)
University of Quindío
Armenia, Colombia

ISSN 1865-0929   ISSN 1865-0937 (electronic)
Communications in Computer and Information Science
ISBN 978-3-031-36356-6   ISBN 978-3-031-36357-3 (eBook)
https://doi.org/10.1007/978-3-031-36357-3

This Springer imprint is published by the registered company Springer Nature Switzerland AG
The registered company address is: Gewerbestrasse 11, 6330 Cham, Switzerland

Preface

The 16th edition of the Colombian Congress of Computing (16CCC) was held in the city of Armenia, Quindío, from October 17 to 21, 2022, within the framework of CLEI 2022. The event was organized by the Colombian Society of Computing and the University of Quindío, aiming to create a space for exchanging ideas, techniques, methodologies, and tools, promoting synergy between researchers, professionals, students, and companies related to the Congress's topics of interest.

The conference took place in person for its sixteenth edition, with a few virtual article presentations that enabled the attendees to participate in the paper discussions, join keynote lectures, and view various workshops.

This book brings together a collection of papers that were presented at the conference, covering a wide range of topics related to computer science. These topics include software engineering and IT architecture, human-computer interaction, cybersecurity and information security, image processing and computer vision, multimedia, artificial intelligence and robotics, education and ICT, data, information and knowledge, distributed systems and large-scale computing, and formal methods in computer systems, among others. The contributions in this book provide valuable insights into the latest research and developments in the field of computer science, and will be of interest to researchers, students, and professionals alike.

The 16th edition of the Colombian Congress of Computing received 40 submissions through its call for papers, out of which 14 were selected for inclusion in this book, although two declined to be published. The review process was carried out by at least three national and international reviewers, ensuring the quality of the selected papers.

We thank the members of our Program Committee for their work and contribution to the success of our conference. Thanks also go to the authors for their submissions, to the organizers, and to Springer, who over the past years, have allowed us to gather the best papers for this book.

May 2023

Vanessa Agredo-Delgado
Pablo H. Ruiz
William J. Giraldo
Alexandra Ruiz
María L. Villegas

Organization

Program Committee members

Andres Moreno	Universidad Central de Venezuela, Venezuela
Andres Moreno	Pontificia Universidad Javeriana, Colombia
Angela Villota Gomez	Universidad Icesi, Colombia
Angela Carrillo	Pontificia Universidad Javeriana, Colombia
Antonio Silva Sprock	Universidad Central de Venezuela, Venezuela
Bell Manrique	Universidad de Medellín, Colombia
Carlos Zapata	Universidad Nacional de Colombia, Colombia
Cecilia Flores	UFCSPA, Brazil
Cesar Collazos	Universidad del Cauca, Colombia
Daniel Correa Botero	Universidad Nacional de Colombia, Colombia
Dario José Delgado	Universidad Nacional Abierta y a Distancia, Colombia
Diana Janeth Lancheros-Cuesta	Universidad de la Salle, Colombia
Edwin Puertas	Universidad Tecnológica de Bolívar, Colombia
Emilcy Juliana Hernández Leal	Universidad de Medellín - Universidad Nacional de Colombia, Colombia
Emilio Insfran	Universitat Politècnica de València, Spain
Enrique Gonzalez	Universidad Javeriana, Colombia
Faber Giraldo	Universidad del Quindío, Colombia
Federico Barber	Universitat Politècnica de València, Spain
Félix Fernández-Peña	Universidad Técnica de Ambato, Colombia
Gabriel Ramirez	Universidad de Medellín, Colombia
Gerardo M. Sarria M.	Pontificia Universidad Javeriana Cali, Colombia
Germán Osorio	Universidad Nacional de Colombia, Colombia
Gloria Piedad Gasca	Universidad de Medellin, Colombia
Grissa Maturana	Universidad Nacional de Colombia, Colombia
Gustavo Isaza	Universidad de Caldas, Colombia
Heitor Costa	Federal University of Lavras, Brazil
Ivan Cabezas	Universidad San Buenaventura de Cali, Colombia
Jairo Enrique Serrano	Universidad Tecnológica de Bolívar, Colombia
Jefferson Arango	Universidad de Caldas, Colombia
Jesús Aranda	Universidad del Valle, Colombia
Jheimer Julian Sepulveda Lopez	Universidad Nacional Abierta y a Distancia, Colombia
Jhon Sanchez Obando	Universidad Nacional de Colombia, Colombia

John Branch	Universidad Nacional de Colombia, Colombia
Jorge Luis Bacca Acosta	Fundación Universitaria Konrad Lorenz, Colombia
Jorge Ernersto Espinosa Oviedo	Politécnico Colombiano Jaime Isaza Cadavid, Colombia
Jose Bocanegra	Pontificia Universidad Javeriana, Colombia
Juan Carlos Martinez Santos	Universidad Tecnológica de Bolívar, Colombia
Julian Moreno	Universidad Nacional de Colombia, Colombia
Julio Hurtado	Universidad del Cauca, Colombia
Julio César Chavarro Porras	Universidad Tecnológica de Pereira, Colombia
Kelly Garces Pernett	Universidad de los Andes, Colombia
Lina Sepulveda	Universidad de Medellin, Colombia
Luis Fernando Castillo Ossa	Universidad de Caldas, Colombia
María Clara Gómez	Universidad de Medellín, Colombia
Marta Tabares	Universidad EAFIT, Colombia
Mauricio Alba-Castro	Universidad Autónoma de Manizales, Colombia
Mauricio Orozco-Alzate	Universidad Nacional de Colombia, Colombia
Miguel Rojas	Universidad Nacional de Colombia, Colombia
Néstor Darío Duque Méndez	Universidad Nacional de Colombia, Colombia
Nicolás Cardozo	Universidad de los Andes, Colombia
Olga Marino	Universidad de los Andes, Colombia
Pablo Torres-Carrion	Universidad Técnica Particular de Loja, Ecuador
Patricia Jaques	Universidad de Vale do Rio dos Sinos, Brazil
Raul Herrera	Universidad de Tarapacá, Chile
Robinson Andrey Duque	Universidad del Valle, Colombia
Robson Fidalgo	Universidade Federal de Pernambuco, Brazil
Roberto Mauricio Cárdenas Cárdenas	Universidad Abierta A Distancia, Colombia
Sandra Cano	Pontificia Universidad Católica de Valparaíso, Chile, Chile
Sebastián Gomez	Tecnológico de Antioquia, Colombia
Sergio Cardona	Universidad del Quindío, Colombia
Tiago Primo	Federal University of Pelotas, Brazil
Valentina Tabares Morales	Universidad Nacional de Colombia, Colombia
Vanessa-Agredo Delgado	Unicomfacauca, Colombia
Vicente Julian	Universitat Politècnica de València, Spain
Wilson Sarmiento	Universidad Militar Nueva Granada, Spain

Academic Committee President

William Joseph Giraldo Orozco	Universidad del Quindío, Colombia

Program Committee President

María Lili Villegas Ramírez   Universidad del Quindío, Colombia

Editorial Committee

Vanessa Agredo-Delgado   Corporación Universitaria Comfacauca
                                Unicomfacauca and Universidad del Cauca,
                                Colombia
Pablo H. Ruiz   Corporación Universitaria Comfacauca
                                Unicomfacauca and Universidad del Cauca,
                                Colombia
Alexandra Ruiz Gaona Ramírez   Universidad del Quindío, Colombia
María Lili Villegas Ramírez   Universidad del Quindío, Colombia
William Joseph Giraldo Orozco   Universidad del Quindío, Colombia

Contents

AlzRastreo: Accompanying Alzheimer's Patients and Their Caregivers

Antonio Silva Sprock[(✉)] [ID] and Ana Morales Bezeira

Escuela de Computación, Universidad Central de Venezuela, Caracas, Venezuela
antonio.m.silva@ucv.ve, ana.morales@ciens.ucv.ve

Abstract. Spatial disorientation is one of the most characteristic symptoms associated with Alzheimer's disease. It manifests as an intense need for the person to go somewhere else, usually with no idea where. This, together with difficulties in recognizing familiar places, highlights the dangers that these patients may face. In this special degree work, the development of a multiplatform mobile application is implemented as a solution to this problem, and thus assists and improves the quality of life of people with Alzheimer's disease and their caregivers. In this sense, we developed the mobile application developed is based on geolocation and its main objective is to allow knowing the location of these patients through the location services of mobile devices, in addition to the definition of geographic areas considered safe, such as their home or work, to notify the relevant caregivers of their whereabouts in case the patients are away from a safe place, and thus provide assistance in case of a possible emergency. The mobile application proposed as a result of this work follows an adaptation of the agile methodology called Mobile-D. It is built under the Android platform, using Apache Cordova and Ionic for its development.

Keywords: mobile app · Alzheimer's disease · Mobile-D · geolocation

1 Introduction

Alzheimer's disease is one of the leading causes of death in older adults in the world and the most common form of dementia [1]. It is a neurodegenerative disease, characterized by beginning with a slow deterioration of memory functions, and progressively, other brain functions. As a consequence of this loss of cognitive functions, Alzheimer's disease culminates in death for those who suffer from it, usually between 3 and 9 years of diagnosis [2]. Some of the symptoms include memory loss, behavioral problems, hallucinations, delusions, and tendencies to wander, get lost, and not find your way home [3]. Although scientists continue to study the disease in search of its causes and cure, also investigations arise to provide better care and quality of life to these patients [1–4].

In this way, technology provides great relief not only for people who have this disease but also for their caregivers or protectors. Likewise, technological advances have led to an increase in devices and applications whose main purpose is to provide these patients

V. Agredo-Delgado et al. (Eds.): CCC 2022, CCIS 1775, pp. 1–14, 2023.
https://doi.org/10.1007/978-3-031-36357-3_1

with a safer and more independent life, and their caregivers with tools that assist with the work of caring for them [1, 4, 5].

These assistive technologies promise to help with a variety of problems, including language, hearing, and vision problems, in addition to supporting these people in daily activities, offering monitoring capabilities, tracking, automated warnings and reminders, location and communication, and even social participation [6]. Those of location and communication, offer patients greater security when walking, find their way without getting lost, and it is possible for them to notify their caregivers of any emergency.

In this sense, the problem of spatial disorientation is one of the most discussed topics through technology. Although innovations regarding geospatial technologies have led to the creation of dedicated locator devices [4, 6], however, the use of this type of assistive technology can become quite expensive, especially if they are complex devices and sophisticated.

As an alternative, exist applications that use geolocation units integrated with mobile devices as a way to monitor and track the location of patients, offering solutions to patients and mainly to caregivers. However, many of these systems have certain limitations:

- They aren't autonomous and are linked to a web app that manages them
- They are proprietary software
- They haven't updated to new versions of the Mobile Operating Systems
- They don't use the map functionality for tracking patients
- Some are only available for use in developed countries.

In addition to this, in countries like Venezuela, there is a lack "(…) of a care policy for the elderly (…) When we individualize those over 80 years of age, we have a population where about 25% have some form of disability, dementia and the most frequent is Alzheimer's" [7]. This situation not only impacts the quality of life of people who suffer from the disease, but also the quality of the entire circle of their families and caregivers.

In this way, the following question arises: it is possible to have a mobile application that makes it easier for caregivers of patients with Alzheimer's to stay informed at all times of their location within safe areas, monitor several patients at the same time, generate timely alerts to through different channels to caregivers and that is not tied to limitations such as country of use and free license for download and use, as well as updated to emerging versions of the Android OS, thereby improving the quality of care they receive and your safety.

Thus, this work shows the development of a mobile application called AlzRastreo, as an alternative to the problem of spatial disorientation suffered by people with Alzheimer's disease and as an alternative to existing solutions. Specifically, in the following sections, the state of the art of mobile applications for the monitoring and tracking of patients with Alzheimer's is shown, the developed system is shown, emphasizing its architecture, the development environment, and methodology, the modules created, the tests carried out and finally the conclusions of the work.

2 State of the Art

As mentioned above, there are mobile applications that use geolocation to monitor and track patients, offering solutions to patients and especially caregivers. These applications include Tweri, Alzheimer Patient - Caretaker, Comfort Zone, and Map4map.

Tweri is a mobile solution developed by the Spanish company Solusoft, which provides positional monitoring and allows Alzheimer's patients to leave the house autonomously [8]. This application allows for the establishment of safe limits, based on the maximum time that the user can be away from home, or the maximum distance radius that is allowed to be away from home [9]. Before leaving, the application must be activated, and when the maximum time or distance is exceeded, the registered caregiver is automatically alerted via email, with the most recent geographical position obtained by the device. Additionally, it has an emergency button that the patient can press at any time [9].

Tweri is not compatible with new versions of Android, is compatible with iOS, and works in conjunction with the Web application for user registration, so it is not a stand-alone application.

Alzheimer Patient and Alzheimer Caretaker are two Android applications that provide assistance services to caregivers and patients, developed as a project by the Department of Information and Communication Technology at the Prince of Songkla University in Thailand. They provide a tracking and monitoring system for users who have Alzheimer's Patients installed [10], and a notification system for those who have Alzheimer Caretaker installed [11].

Another mobile application is ComfortZone [12, 13], based on the OmniLink Focal-Point tracking software [14], which can, through GPS, find devices that can be used to locate people. If a patient leaves the pre-set area in the application, the software sends a text message or an email in a period of 2 and 30 min, with the location of the patient to his caregiver. The length of time depends on the follow-up plan chosen by the patient's caregiver.

ComfortZone additionally offers assistance to the patient's family through a monitoring service center 24 h a day, 7 days a week, and the possibility of access to emergency physicians from the MedicAlert Foundation [15].

Another similar application is Map4map [16], offered free of charge, and like ComfortZone, it sends an alarm to the caregiver's mobile when the patient crosses the pre-established comfort zone.

Table 1 shows a simple comparison of some of the existing applications previously studied and analyzed, found for the monitoring and location of patients with Alzheimer's.

Of the analyzed applications, only two of them are free and free to use, two of them use maps, and all of them are for the Android mobile operating system, however, one of them, which works with maps and is free, does not work with the latest versions of Android.

From the above, the proposal arose to develop a system capable of working with the spatial location, through the device's GPS and maps, free of charge, which can send Push notification messages to the caregiver's mobile device, text messages (SMS) and emails that include access to the patient's location map to caregivers, monitor the location of the patient in real-time and implement the functionality of the help button for the patient in possible situations of dislocation and loss.

Table 1. Comparison of some of the existing applications for monitoring and location of Alzheimer's patients.

Application	Operating System	Functionalities	Free
Tweri	Android IOS	Location map, out-of-zone alarm, emails, stray button, emails	Yes
Alzheimer Patient - Caretaker	Android	Location map, out-of-zone alarm, emails	No
Comfort Zone	Android	Out-of-zone alarm, emails, and SMS	No
Map4map	Android	Out-of-zone alarm	Yes

3   System Developed

We developed the AlzRastreo System using the Mobile-D agile methodology [17–19]. The solution consists of the AlzRastreo mobile application, and a web server that acts as an intermediary between the application and the database. Likewise, among the functionalities of the web server, there is also user authentication, monitoring of user databases, and sending notifications to caregivers.

Next, we describe the methodology used, and we show the architecture of the AlzRastreo System, the environment, and the modules developed.

3.1   Methodology

We used the Mobile-D agile methodology [17–19] which provides tools and practices that best suit the planning and design of applications, especially those projects with short development periods and with a small development team, since it especially focuses on overcoming the challenges associated with mobile developments. In Fig. 1 we show the phases of the Mobile-D methodology.

Fig. 1. Methodology used. Adaptation of [18].

In the exploration phase [19], we did the initial planning and establishment of the project. In this phase, we define the requirements, scope, and development environment of AlzRastreo. In the Initialization phase, we prepare the development environment, analyze the requirements, refine the planning, and specify the AlzRastreo modules.

During the Production phase, we implemented the functionalities and requirements defined in the previous phases, including the implementation of the System. During production, we used an iterative and incremental development cycle [19], in addition to using test-driven development [18]. We used the plan-work-release process, and we repeated it iteratively until we completed all the functionalities. Our first activity was to plan the task of determining requirements, and the tasks to be carried out. Previously, we prepare the iteration tests (that is why the technique has the name Test-Driven Development, TDD [20, 21]).

We executed the tasks on working days. In the Stabilize phase, we integrated all the AlzRastreo modules and develop the final documentation of the application. Finally, in the testing phase, it was possible to evaluate that AlzRastreo implemented the required functionalities, this phase also allowed the debugging of errors in the application.

3.2 System Architecture

AlzRastreo uses geospatial information, obtained through location services integrated into the operating systems of the mobile devices on which it runs. AlzRastreo uses this information to inform caregivers of the location of patients. Also, send push notifications when the patient leaves the defined safe zone so that the caregiver can assist in the event of a potential emergency.

The application defined Safe Zones, which are the geographical area with a specific radius that demarcates a real location where patients are safe. The caregivers must define these safe zones in the App, and these can be nearby areas to homes, jobs, etc.

Together with the mobile application, a Web server running in the background is necessary, whose objective is to establish a connection between the application and the central database, where the data generated by the users will be stored, as a form of monitoring. We show the architecture of the system in Fig. 2.

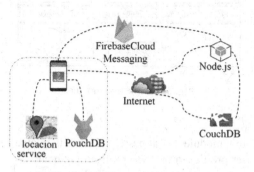

Fig. 2. AlzRastreo architecture.

AlzRastreo works together with a Node.js Web server that acts as an intermediary between the mobile application and the CouchDB database. Likewise, among the functionalities of the Web server, there is also user authentication, monitoring of user databases, and sending notifications to users. The System establishes this connection to the server via the Internet and uses the phone's location services as well as a local PouchDB database. Also, the System used the Push notification mechanisms, with the server and connection to Google's Firebase Cloud Messaging.

3.3 Development Environment

We developed the application using Ionic version 1.2, AngularJS version 1.4.6, and Apache Cordova version 6.5.0. We built the server on top of Node.js version 7.9.0, and the framework for Node.js was Express.js version 4.15.2. The database server used was CouchDB version 1.6.1 and for the local database of the devices, we worked with PouchDB version 5.4.5.

3.4 Developed Modules

We structured AlzRastreo into 7 modules to satisfy the requirements defined in the exploration phase of the Mobile-D methodology [17]. The modules make up two planes: The Frontend, which are the user interface modules (Authentication, Patient, and Caregiver), and the Backend which covers all the internal functionalities of the application and communicates with the user interfaces. Figure 3 shows the model of the AlzRastreo System.

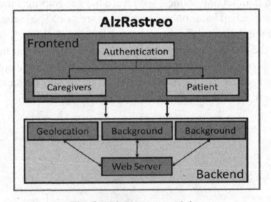

Fig. 3. AlzRastreo modules.

1) **Authentication**: this module encompasses all aspects related to the authentication of the different user profiles in the system; from login and registration to password recovery in case it has been forgotten. Similarly, this module allows defining the types of users of the application, and how the system distinguishes them to provide the different functionalities inherent to each type. The defined user profiles are patient and caregiver. Figure 4 shows the interfaces of this module.

2) **Patient:** where the system implements the functionalities and services necessary for patient-type users. It also involves the services that allow the synchronization between the local and remote databases, and the requests to the AlzRastreo server, as well as the implementation of the requirements specified in the exploration phase.

Among the main requirements implemented are the interfaces that indicate to the patient if he is geographically located within a safe zone, and screen alerts if the patient leaves a safe zone. This module also allows the patients to see their caregivers defined, as well as the safe areas defined.

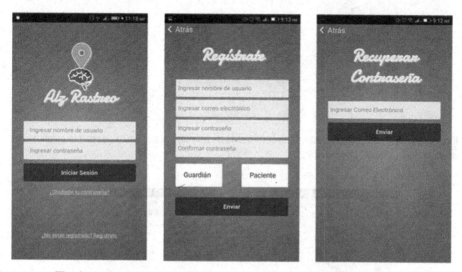

Fig. 4. Authentication interface (start session, register, password recovery).

Figure 5 shows a subset of the interfaces associated with this module. First, the initial patient user interface after the authentication of the application, which will show the map with its safe coverage radius colored in purple, in case it is within this safe zone; then the initial interface of the patient type user is displayed once he has authenticated himself in the application, and he is outside some secure geographical zone.

Then the map and a notification in a red box will be displayed alerting the situation. Finally, Fig. 5 shows the initial interface for the patient after he does authentication in the application, and even his caregiver has not configured safe zones for him.

3) **Caregiver:** in this module, we structured all the functionalities for the type of user called caregiver. Among the main functionalities determined in the exploration phase and implemented in this module are: displaying the list of patients associated with a caregiver and selecting a patient, being able to from another interface, and displaying the geographic location information of the same (a caregiver can have more than one patient in your care).

Figure 6 shows the interface to select the patient and display its current location. Figure 7 shows the invitations received for the caregiver to accept patients and manage the list of patients. Figure 8 shows the administration interface for safe

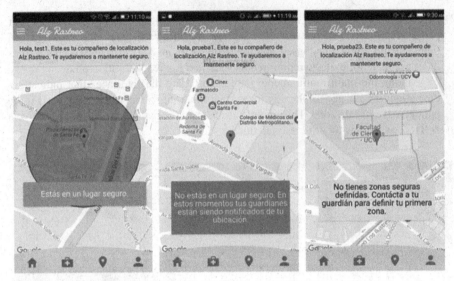

Fig. 5. Start interface for the patient user (when he is in a safe zone; when he isn´t in a safe zone; when he hasn´t a safe zone defined).

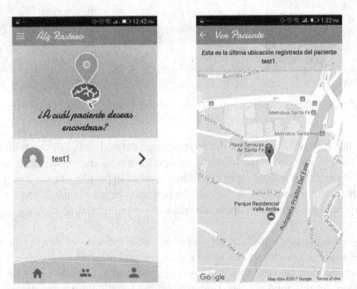

Fig. 6. Start interface for caregivers where the system shows the patient list, and the patient location named test1.

zones associated with a patient. Finally, in this module, it is also possible to have a caregiver with special "Primary Caregiver" privileges, who has access to a list of all the caregivers associated with a particular patient (see Fig. 9) and can add or delete caregivers to that patient.

This primary caregiver can perform these actions by searching for caregivers in a special bar, which filters caregiver-type users and sends an invitation to the patient to accept it. In addition, she may assign her primary caregiver privilege to any other caregiver agreed to by the patient.

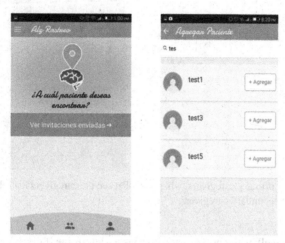

Fig. 7. Caregiver's interface where he must see the pendent invitations for becoming caregiver, and the list of his patients.

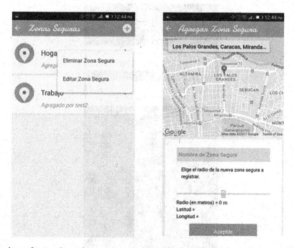

Fig. 8. Caregiver interface where he must see the safe zones of his patient, and he must add new safe zones for his patients.

4) **Geolocation**: this module handles the location objects of the users obtained from the mobile device, as well as the connection with the Google Maps API for its correct display on the maps. Here, we implemented the necessary tools for the construction of safe zones through a given radius in meters (the caregiver can configure this

Fig. 9. Interface for primary caregivers, where he must see the caregivers list related to a patient, and the erase of the secondary caregiver.

parameter), as well as the necessary formulas to determine if given the longitude and latitude of a user's location, it is or is not within a safe zone (see Fig. 10).

Fig. 10. Geolocation interface which runs in the background in the smartphone.

5) **Background:** in this module, we implemented the services necessary for the application to continue running as a background process on the mobile device.
6) **Push Notifications:** this module involves the management of push notifications sent from the AlzRastreo server to caregivers and patients when the patient leaves a safe

area, likewise, this module also involves the registration of devices for the operation of these notifications. Figure 11 shows the arrival of location notifications in the Caregiver App.

7) **Web server:** in this module, we implemented the web server that works as an intermediary between the requests of the mobile application and the CouchDB database server. At the same time, it also provides the necessary functionalities for the development of the events that allow the server to monitor the database updates; and in this way make the pertinent notifications. The server sends the notifications via email to the caregivers.

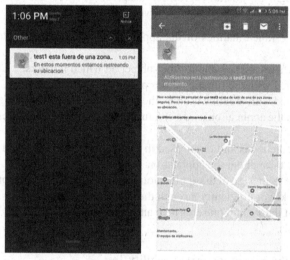

Fig. 11. Push notification for the caregiver when the patient leaves the safe zone, and his location on the map.

4   Tests

The Mobile-D methodology indicates two types of tests, those functionalities and of acceptance and usability.

4.1   Functionality Testing

Carried out throughout the development of the System and finally tested each one of the requirements and functionalities of the developed modules, such as user registration, login, accept caregiver invitation, add caregiver and view caregivers (these last 3 for patient users), send invitation to the patient, search patient, add patient and view patients (for caregiver users), add, delete and edit safe zones, add caregivers to a patient and assign primary caregiver to another caregiver (for caregiver users).

4.2 Usability and Acceptance Test

Regarding these tests, we used a survey as an evaluation instrument, applied to 10 people from different professions. They had different knowledge in the area of computing, and especially the development of mobile applications. They were two Mechanical Engineers, two Computer Science graduates, web developers, a Chemical Engineer, and an Electronic Engineer, a mobile application developer. The other four people were two old housewives, and two students from the Central University of Venezuela.

We used the Likert scale to measure and know the degree of conformity of the users of the application. This scale evaluates each response value as follows: (1) strongly disagree, (2) disagree, (3) neither agree nor disagree, (4) agree, and (5) strongly agree.

Below we show the questions of the survey

1. We present the functionalities of the application (login, register, add patient, etc.) intuitively.
2. The user interfaces are suitable for the subject on which it works.
3. You are satisfied with the functionalities provided by the application.
4. You are satisfied with the time used by the application to perform the functionalities.
5. Considers that the application uses a common language through phrases, terminology, and concepts.
6. Consider that the icons and terms used in the different interfaces and menus remain homogeneous throughout the application.
7. Considers that the design of the application is an aid and allows functions to be carried out more quickly or efficiently through the use of shortcuts.
8. Considers that the system presents help and documentation necessary for the correct use of the tools.

4.3 Results of the Acceptance and Usability Test

After applying the survey, we obtained favorable results, which show usability and acceptance by users, as reflected in Fig. 12.

The best-evaluated question turned out to be the first, where 100% of the respondents indicated that they strongly agreed. In question 2, nine people (90%) strongly agreed and one person agreed. 50%, that is, five people indicated that they strongly agreed with the third question, while four (40%) agreed and only one person neither agreed nor disagreed. The fourth question was answered by four people (40%) strongly in agreement, five people (50%) in agreement, and one neither in agreement nor in disagreement. In the fifth and sixth questions, eight people (80%) answered strongly in agreement, and two (20%) in agreement. In the seventh question, 60% (six people) strongly agree, 30% agree, and maybe only one person neither agrees nor disagrees finally the eighth and last questions, were evaluated as disagreeing by one person, five people agreeing and four people strongly agreeing.

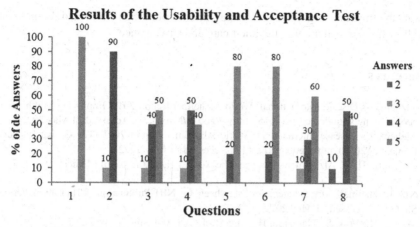

Fig. 12. Results of the usability and acceptance test for AlzRastreo.

5 Conclusions

The AlzRastreo application works as an alternative solution for locating people, providing its users with more security, by avoiding the risks involved in spatial disorientation in patients with Alzheimer's. This application also notifies their caregivers when they are far from a safe zone, and provides tools to locate them and, in this way, find them.

The application also provides the possibility for caregivers to monitor more than one patient at a time. This functionality is extremely attractive with a view to the app being adopted by institutions or medical care service companies that can help in the care of patients suffering from the disease.

We applied the usability and acceptance test, and we could demonstrate that the AlzRastreo is usable, intuitive, and has a simple user interface, which is specifically focused on older people and their caregivers. This provides ease when using all the features it provides, especially the panic button.

It was also possible to implement all the development of notifications to caregiver users by email and push notifications, to alert them when their loved ones or patients are out of a safe place. Likewise, we developed a web server, which works as an intermediary between the database and the mobile application, to execute the aforementioned notifications when appropriate.

Even so, the application can implement other features and improvements in future works. These new functionalities will be the creation of a web portal that shows patients on a map, and also functionalities to determine the speed of the patients in their movement, as well as the direction in which they are heading.

In the future, usability and acceptance tests will also be carried out on medical-health personnel or institutions specializing in this type of disease to obtain more specialized opinions and suggestions for improvements associated with the health and well-being of the patient.

AlzRastreo is a solution not only for the location and monitoring of patients with Alzheimer's but also an interesting solution for the peace of mind of caregivers who most of the time are forgotten when taking into account their needs and requirements that allow them to better carry way their care and surveillance.

References

1. Alzheimer's Disease International: World Alzheimer Report 2016: Improving healthcare for people living with dementia (2016). https://goo.gl/MoxPCW. Accessed 21 May 2022
2. Alzheimer's Disease International: World Alzheimer Report 2015: The Global Impact of Dementia (2015). http://goo.gl/HXf5Pu. Accessed 21 May 2022
3. Querfurth, H.W.: Alzheimer's Disease. The New England Journal of Medicine, pp. 329–344 (2010)
4. NIA: Alzheimer's disease genetics fact sheet. In: NIH Publication (2011). https://goo.gl/S8pCPx. Accessed 21 May 2022
5. Maurer, K., Volk, S., Gerbaldo, H.: Auguste D and Alzheimer's disease. The Lancet (349), 1546–1549 (1997). https://doi.org/10.1016/S0140-6736(96)10203-8
6. Alzheimer's Association: ComfortZone – Technology 101 (2016). https://goo.gl/6zvxQV. Accessed 20 May 2022
7. Andara, A.: Venezuela todavía carece de políticas de atención al adulto con Alzheimer, advierte especialista. Efecto Cocuyo (2022). https://efectococuyo.com/la-humanidad/venezuela-todavia-carece-de-politicas-de-atencion-al-adulto-con-alzheimer-advierte-especialista/
8. Tweri: ¿WhatisTweti?. http://goo.gl/a7oguU. Accessed 2 Apr 2022
9. Google Play: Ttweri Alzheimer Caregiver Tool. https://goo.gl/IaiFev. Accessed 24 Apr 2022
10. Google Play: Alzheimer Patient. https://goo.gl/7rAj9x. Accessed 5 May 2022
11. Google Play: Alzheimer Caretaker. https://goo.gl/Um85tB. Accessed 5 May 2022
12. Alzheimer's Association: Comfort Zone. https://goo.gl/AfonZh. Accessed 5 May 2022
13. Comfort Zone. https://goo.gl/3jfWVS. Accessed 5 MAy 2022
14. Omnilink Mobile Applications: https://goo.gl/VNnJRu. Accessed 5 May 2022
15. MedicAlert Foundation: https://www.medicalert.org/. Accessed 5 May 2022
16. Centro de Referencia Estatal de atención a personas con enfermedad de Alzheimer y otras demencias: CATÁLOGO: Alzhéimer's Apps (2014), https://goo.gl/Eq9uyU. Accessed 5 May 2022
17. Abrahamsson, P., et al.: Mobile-D: an agile approach for mobile application development. In: Companion to the 19th Annual ACM SIGPLAN Conference on Object-Oriented Programming Systems, Languages, and Applications OOPSLA '04, pp. 174–175 (2004). https://doi.org/10.1145/1028664.1028736
18. Mahmood, S., Lu, J.: An investigation into mobile based approach for healthcare activities, occupational therapy system. International Conference on Software Engineering Research and Practice SERP13, pp. 95–101 (2013)
19. Agile Software Technologies Research Programme: Mobile-D. http://goo.gl/4fFFis. Accessed 5 May 2022
20. Beck, K.: Test-Driven Development: by example. Addison-Wesley Professional (2003)
21. Astels, D.: Test driven development: A practical guide. Prentice Hall Professional Technical Reference (2003)

Application of Artificial Intelligence Techniques for Cancer Data Analysis in Brazil

Santiago Tabares-Morales[1]([⊠]) [iD], Néstor Darío Duque-Méndez[1] [iD],
Marta Rosecler Bez[2] [iD], Valentina Tabares-Morales[1] [iD],
and Juliano Varella de Carvalho[2] [iD]

[1] Universidad Nacional de Colombia – Sede, Manizales, Colombia
{satabaresmo,ndduqueme,vtabaresm}@unal.edu.co
[2] Universidade Feevale – Novo, Hamburgo, Brasil
{martabez,julianovc}@feevale.br

Abstract. The application of Artificial Intelligence techniques, specifically Machine Learning, in large volumes of data in the health area, is revolutionizing the way some complex tasks are carried out, since the results obtained can support decision-making. In this work, different Machine Learning algorithms were applied to medical data from the Brazilian National Cancer Institute (INCA) since 1985, in order to generate a model that would allow predicting the possible result of a first oncological treatment. Previously, an analysis of the different datasets is carried out, as well as processing tasks. In order to facilitate the visualization of the different variables, an interactive dashboard was created. The results, being preliminary, open space for new works.

Keywords: data analysis · machine learning · cancer

1 Introduction

According to the World Health Organization (WHO), cancer is one of the leading causes of death worldwide [1]. This is a problem of interest to many communities since efforts are required from different areas of knowledge to find strategies to minimize the negative effect, preventing and controlling the different types of cancer is a priority worldwide.

Specifically in the Brazilian context, which is of special interest for this work, there is a high number of cancer cases, especially prostate and breast cancer. The National Cancer Institute (INCA) of Brazil is responsible for collecting information on this disease, essential for research and planning of programs for its control. This allows knowing about trends, risk factors and the effect of prevention actions, early detection, treatment and palliative care [2].

Currently, there is a large number of Artificial Intelligence (AI) techniques that are applied in different contexts and areas of knowledge, particularly when it comes to working with large amounts of data, a branch of AI appears that is Machine Learning or Learning Automatic. It corresponds to the study of algorithms that learn and improve through experience. The learning process is based on two phases, the first is the estimation

V. Agredo-Delgado et al. (Eds.): CCC 2022, CCIS 1775, pp. 15–27, 2023.
https://doi.org/10.1007/978-3-031-36357-3_2

of unknown relationships from a set of data and the second uses those relationships to predict new outputs of the system [3].

From these phases, the two main types of Machine Learning arise, which are Supervised Learning and Unsupervised Learning [3, 4]. There are several algorithms used to apply these techniques, some of interest for this work are: Linear Regression, Linear Discriminant Analysis, K Nearest Neighbors (KNN), Decision Trees, Random Forest, Support Vector Machines and Networks Neural [3, 5–7].

It is stated that computer systems that support the decision-making process and that are based on Machine Learning have high potential and specifically in the medical area, it is considered that they can revolutionize the way complex tasks that require of specialists, supporting their work to increase precision in diagnoses and treatments [4]. *Machine Learning* techniques offer alternatives that were not available before and that allow conclusions to be reached through different investigations that contribute to the global fight against diseases such as cancer that affects the entire population [8].

In the literature, a large number of works are identified in which data collected in different areas of health are used and in which artificial intelligence techniques are applied in order to obtain hidden patterns [9], improve visualization for decision making [10], identify features strongly linked to certain diagnoses [11] and generate applications with validated models [7]. In addition, in the specific case of data associated with cancer, proposals are identified in which Machine Learning techniques are applied to different types of cancer such as prostate, breast and oral cancer [8, 12, 13]. Although many investigations have been carried out in this regard, there are still open spaces associated with the treatment of this data, improvement of the algorithms, analysis of the results and mechanisms for their visualization.

The objective of this work was the application of AI techniques in medical datasets from the National Cancer Institute of Brazil (INCA) from 1985 to 2020 in order to identify patterns that initially allow predicting results related to cancer treatments applied for different types of cancer. The rest of the document is organized as follows: Sect. 2 shows the methodology adopted and the steps taken; Then, in Sect. 3, the results and discussion are presented, to finally reach Sect. 4 where the conclusions and future work are presented.

2   Methodology

2.1   Data Origin – INCA Dataset

With the data provided by INCA, access is given to a national database which has records from the year 1985 to 2020 (except for the year 1987 for which there are no data), where the information is anonymized of each patient diagnosed with cancer in the year of their first consultation. The databases are constantly updated, and the last update was made with the data received by the RHC Integrator, which is a web system developed by INCA to consolidate data from Hospital Cancer Registries (RHC) throughout Brazil, from 16/09/2021 to 04/12/2022. All RHC data is available at inca.gov.br.

There is a total of 34 different datasets. They are all made up of the same 44 attributes, which contain medical and socioeconomic information on each of the patients. Available variables include: age, sex, state of birth, level of schooling, date of first consultation, type of cancer, diagnostic test, first treatment received, state after first treatment.

One of the main problems with these data is that the state of São Paulo does not deliver all the data to the RHC, therefore, several patients corresponding to this state present attributes with "Uninformed" or null values.

The datasets vary greatly in the number of samples taken per year, as can be seen in Table 1, where it is observed that in the first years an efficient registry of cancer patients in the country was not kept. From the year 2000, a significant increase in the number of samples per dataset is seen. Although the number of records increased, there is also a great tendency to have atypical values that in most cases corresponded to values that can be attributed to errors when uploading the information to the INCA databases.

Table 1. Number of data per year INCA

Year	Patients	Year	Patients	Year	Patients
1985	1	1997	146	2009	221099
1986	1	1998	1269	2010	241280
1987	0	1999	3334	2011	259492
1988	3	2000	71268	2012	263891
1989	3	2001	91720	2013	281580
1990	4	2002	104760	2014	292931
1991	6	2003	112378	2015	597387
1992	10	2004	126390	2016	299939
1993	18	2005	150271	2017	303512
1994	27	2006	156604	2018	263216
1995	38	2007	177564	2019	166703
1996	55	2008	200086	2020	124053

2.2 Data Preparation

Most of the variables are of the categorical type where many have values of "Uninformed" or null, which were eliminated. To facilitate the application of Machine Learning algorithms, the categorical variables are converted into ordinal integers, for the date-type characteristics the same process was carried out, only for these it was filtered by valid dates.

A NaN value has been set for all fields that have a label of "Uninformed" or a null value, in order to be able to eliminate or replace these values. Unfortunately, some of the features have quite high amounts of NaN values, such as the case of HISTFAMC where there are 60% missing values. This makes the use of an algorithm for imputation to establish the missing values infeasible and removes some of the attributes from the datasets.

This process was carried out on all the datasets, but in order to show an example, Fig. 1 presents the results obtained for the 2020 dataset, where a correlation matrix was generated with some of the attributes.

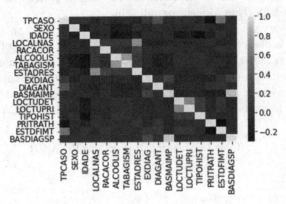

Fig. 1. Correlation matrix dataset 2020

In this 2020 dataset, despite having a large number of attributes, there is also a large number of "Uninformed" values that force us to dispense with records that could contribute to the process, however, the preprocessed data allows valuable knowledge to be extracted. In the cleaning process, it was changed from 124,053 records to 16,627 and from 44 characteristics including the class to 17.

After performing an exploratory analysis on the datasets of the last years, it was decided to generate 4 different datasets for the application of *Machine Learning* algorithms. These were divided into: Most recent *dataset* corresponding to 2020 (D2020), the last 5 years concatenated (D5AÑOS), the 2020 *dataset* by performing a balancing on the values of the classes sought to be predicted (DB2020) and the last 5 years balanced (DB5AÑOS).

For dataset balancing, the Oversampling or Subsampling strategies were analyzed. In this case we chose to use Oversampling, which consists of adding "synthetic" data from the minority class to increase its weight over the total dataset. This strategy uses Imbalanced-learn, which is an open-source library, with MIT license, based on scikit-learn and provides tools when dealing with classification with unbalanced classes, specifically using the RamdomOverSampler class to perform a random subsampling of the majority classes by choosing random samples with or without replacement.

2.3 Data Visualization

When working with large volumes of data, it is important to offer possibilities to visualize them more easily. From this need arises data visualization techniques, which play a very important role by allowing, through images and graphics, to make them more understandable, attractive, manageable and useful, allowing multidimensional analysis [14]. Before eliminating the values without information, a dashboard was made to allow a better understanding of the data, because having such a high number of attributes can be counterproductive for the analysis, only some of the attributes that can be more representative are selected, which are: SEXO (patient gender), LOCALNAS (Place of birth), LOCTUDET (CID-O cancer classification), IDADE (Age), ALCOOLIS (Alcoholism history), RACACOR (Race), TABAGISM (Smoking history), PRITRATH (First treatment in hospital), EXDIAG (tests relevant to diagnosis) and ESTDFIMT (Disease status at the end of first treatment).

For the visualization, each year is worked individually. Figure 2 shows the graphs corresponding to the year 2020, which are representative of the other years.

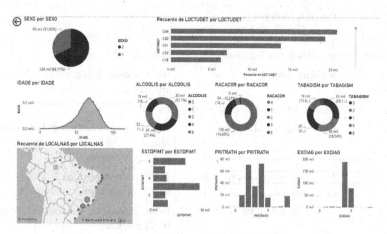

Fig. 2. Dashboard for INCA2020

It is observed that the data cover a large part of the country's population centers. The most common types of cancer are skin cancer (C44), female breast cancer (C50), prostate cancer (C61), cervical cancer (C53) and colon cancer (C18). The average age of the patients is 67 years. There is no predominance in alcohol and tobacco consumption habits.

2.4   Application of Machine Learning Models

After preparing the data and building the dashboard for its visualization, different artificial intelligence algorithms were applied, particularly supervised learning, in order to see the possibility of predicting the final state of a person after performing the test. First cancer treatment, reflected by the characteristic STDFIMT (class).

The first step was a selection of the attributes to work with since the amount of data depends on this, because some columns are eliminated, as well as some rows when having several "no information" values. Both the correlation matrix and the feature importance score (feature_importances) of the model were used to reduce tfeature set.

The attributes that were selected can be seen in detail in Table 2, where the attribute, description and possible values can be observed.

The attribute to be predicted is multiclass whose possible values are: **(0)** No evidence of disease - complete remission, **(1)** Partial remission, **(2)** Stable disease, **(3)** Progressing disease, **(4)** Oncologic therapeutic support, **(5)** Dead.

For this process, the Google Research tool Colab was used, which allows working in Python programming language with its different libraries for the implementation of different *Machine Learning* algorithms, where a partition of the data set of 80% for *training* and 20% for *testing* was carried out.

Table 2. Selected attributes

Attribute	Description	Data type
LOCALNAS	Patient's birth status	State Code
LOCTUDET	Primary tumor location	CID-O code 3 digits
LOCTUPRI	Detailed tumor location	CodeCID-O 4 digits
TABAGISM	Smoking history	Not validated, 5. Not valid, 6. Not applicable
IDADE	Age of patient when diagnosed	Integer
EXDIAG	Relevant diagnostic tests	1. Clinical examination and pathology; 2Imaging tests; 3. Endoscopy and exploratory surgery; 4.
BASDIAGSP	Most important basis for tumor diagnosis	1. Clinical examination 2. Microscopic aids 3. Microscopic confirmation
PRITRATH	First treatment at the Hospital	None; 2. Surgery; 3. Radiation therapy (RXT); 4. Chemotherapy (QT); 5. Hormone therapy (HT); 6. Bone marrow transplantation (BMT); 7. Immunotherapy; 8. Others
ESTADRES	Current state of residence	State Code

3   Results and Discussion

3.1   Results with D2020

With the reduction of samples made when cleaning the dataset, a total of 16,6627 samples were obtained for the year 2020. Different models were run and their performance is compared in a single graph where each of the respective *boxplot is presented in* Fig. 3, whose Y axis corresponds to the percentage of success and on the X axis each of the models using the following acronyms: Linear Regression (LIR), Logistic Regression (LR), Linear Discriminant Analysis (LDA), Gaussian Naive Bayes (NB), K nearest neighbors (KNN), Support Vector Machines (SVM), Gaussian Naive Bayes (NB), Decision Trees (CART), Random Forest (RF), Gradient Boosting Machine (GBM), AdaBoost (ABC), Neural Networks (NN) and Multilayer Perceptron (NN_MLP).

It is observed that all models have a similar behavior, allowing us to conclude that there is no improvement with some a priori more complex algorithms such as Neural

Networks (NN) or Multilayer Neural Networks (NN_MLP). The best performing model is the Gradient Boosting Machine (GBM). In order to improve these values, a reduction of classes was proposed as well as the generation of synthetic data that seeks to balance the classes.

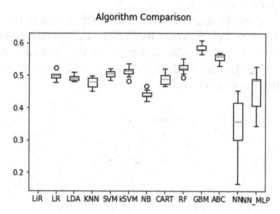

Fig. 3. Boxplot INCA 2020 models

In order to improve the results obtained, the number of ESTDFIMT classes is reduced, 4 groupings are made trying to preserve main characteristics in the classes that are joined. The new class groupings are: **(0)** complete remission, **(1)** partial remission or stable disease, **(2)** disease in progress or oncological therapeutic support, **(3)** dead.

Figure 4 shows the percentage of success on the Y-axis and on the X-axis for each of the models analyzed. It can be seen that the reduction of classes shows a small improvement, but it is not really significant and the general behavior of each of the models executed is maintained.

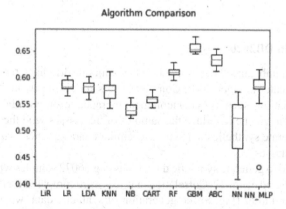

Fig. 4. Boxplot INCA 2020 class reduction models

3.2 Results with D5AÑOS

In order to have a larger amount of data, the datasets of the last 5 years are combined, this allows going from having 16627 to 150938 to apply the different Machine Learning algorithms. For this purpose, the datasets were concatenated from 2016 to 2020, after having performed the respective cleaning in each one.

With this new dataset, the characteristics of the 2020 dataset were preserved despite the fact that, as shown in Fig. 5, where the Y axis corresponds to the percentage of success and the X axis to each of the models analyzed, the results are around 50%, with the Gradient Boosting Classifier (GBM), AdaBoost (ABC) and Random Forest (RF) algorithms delivering the best results.

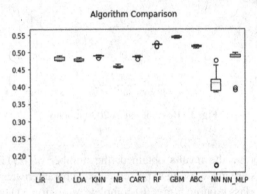

Fig. 5. Boxplot INCA models 5 years

For the GBM model we have the respective confusion matrix (Fig. 6), where each one of the possible classes is shown on the axes. This graph shows that there are problems especially in the minority classes, since the class is the one with the best results and the one with the largest number of samples, so it is necessary to generate new balanced datasets.

3.3 Results with DB2020

Since we have an unbalanced dataset, due to the values of the characteristic we want to predict have a greater number of (0) Complete remission, we have problems to predict less frequent situations such as (4) Oncological therapeutic support. For this, there are two options, which can be to reduce the samples of the classes with the largest amount of data or to generate synthetic data that have similar characteristics to the observations of the minority classes.

It was decided to generate synthetic data, obtaining 36072 samples where each of the classes to be predicted has 6012. Correlation matrices were compared for the same dataset before (Fig. 7) and after (Fig. 8) the generation of synthetic data, where it was found that there is no significant change in the relationship between the different attributes.

The different Machine Learning algorithms are run again, where significant improvements are observed in the performance of some of the algorithms such as KNN, CART

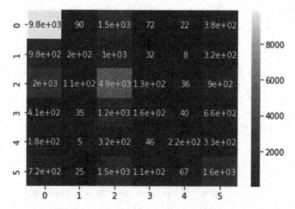

Fig. 6. Matriz de confusión GBC para INCA 5 años

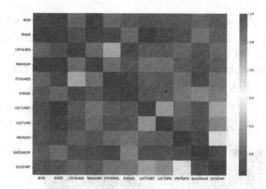

Fig. 7. Unbalanced correlation matrix

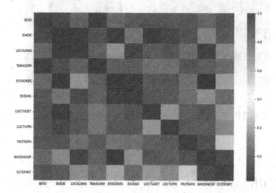

Fig. 8. Balanced correlation matrix

and RF, all of which can be seen in Fig. 9, which shows the percentage of success on the Y axis and on the X axis for each of the models analyzed.

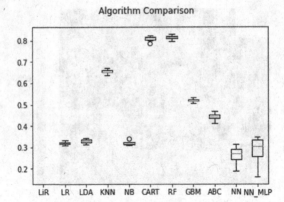

Fig. 9. Boxplot INCA 2020 balanced models

The model with the best results was Random Forest (RF) for which the confusion matrix presented in Fig. 10 is generated, in order to find the performance for each of the classes. A significant improvement was found, reducing the number of errors when confusing the minority classes. This is also evident in the recall for each class: [0.705, 0.82959268, 0.60932203, 0.95409015, 1., 0.85215272].

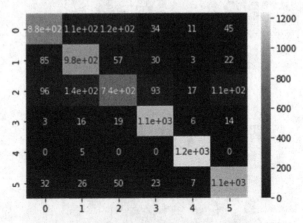

Fig. 10. RF confusion matrix for balanced INCA2020

3.4 Results with DB5AÑOS

Working with the balanced classes and with 59362 samples for each one, we have an increase to 356172 in total. Applying the same algorithms with which we have worked, we conclude that Random Forest generates the best results as can be seen in Fig. 11, which shows on the Y axis the percentage of success and on the X axis each of the analyzed models.

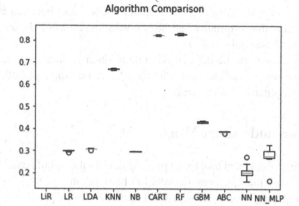

Fig. 11. Boxplot INCA 5 years balanced models

Finally, the confusion matrix for the Random Forest model presented in Fig. 12 is generated, where the behavior of the 2020 *dataset* is preserved, in which it is observed that when balanced, the minority classes show a significant improvement. The *recall* values for each class are: [0.68352297, 0.91043007, 0.65359031, 0.92756506, 0.99127636, 0.87013964].

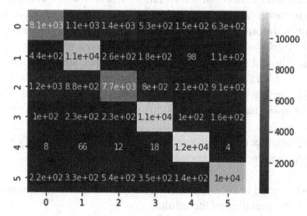

Fig. 12. Balanced 5-year RF INCA confusion matrix

3.5 Discussion

Working with data from the last 5 years and working with data from 2020 generates similar results, possibly due to the distribution of the data, with only small changes in the results of the different models. This behavior was evidenced in the correlation matrices of each of the datasets.

Algorithms such as Decision Trees and Random Forest on balanced *datasets* show a significant improvement, having values of around 80% of success, while working with unbalanced data these same algorithms had a success rate between 50% and 60%. However, algorithms that originally had higher values such as GBM do not show any improvement when balanced.

The minority classes in the dataset generate a much greater error, since the algorithms do not have enough data to work with them, so generating synthetic data allowed extracting more information from them.

4   Conclusions and Future Work

AI techniques are an important tool for improving data analysis, but generally significant data preparation work must be done in order to obtain results.

Models were generated that allow a valid approach to the prediction of the results of the first oncological treatment, especially with the use of Random Forest, where information is obtained that can help both the patient and the health professional to make decisions on the treatment to be performed or not.

The application of data balancing algorithms improves the results of minority classes, helping to ensure their correct classification, since processing with the original data generates a high number of false negatives.

The availability of data is of utmost importance in any area, but it is even more important in health issues, which is why it is important that institutions such as INCA take charge of this data collection, which allows research to be carried out. It is also necessary to try to carry out a better collection process, since in this case, unfortunately, there were many "uninformed" values that could have improved the results obtained.

The use of the *dashboard allows* access to an easy-to-use tool for anyone to visualize the data and possibly find valuable information or generate some probable hypotheses.

As future work, it is expected to replicate this process with Colombian data, in order to generate a comparison regarding the cancer situation in both countries. Work with other *Machine Learning* techniques and modify some other parameters of the techniques used.

In the visualization part, it is proposed as a future work, to modify the tool so that it has the direct option to change between years, as well as being easily accessible to anyone.

Finally, it is expected to socialize the results with the health community in order to generate a better interpretation of the results.

References

1. Organización Mundial de la Salud (OMS): Cáncer. https://www.who.int/es/news-room/fact-sheets/detail/cancer
2. Ministerio de Salud, Instituto Nacional de Cancer (INCA): El cáncer en Brasil (2013)
3. Chopra, R.: Machine Learning. Khanna Publishing House (2020)
4. Kourou, K., Exarchos, T.P., Exarchos, K.P., Karamouzis, M.V., Fotiadis, D.I.: Machine learning applications in cancer prognosis and prediction. Comput. Struct. Biotechnol. J. **13**, 8–17 (2015). https://doi.org/10.1016/j.csbj.2014.11.005

5. Ray, S.: A quick review of machine learning algorithms. Proceedings International Conference Machine Learning Big Data, Cloud Parallel Comput. Trends, Prespectives Prospect. Com., pp. 35–39 (2019). https://doi.org/10.1109/COMITCon.2019.8862451
6. Batta, M.: Machine learning algorithms - a review. Int. J. Sci. Res. IJ. **9**, 381–386 (2020). https://doi.org/10.21275/ART20203995
7. Amador, S., Polo, A., Rotbei, S., Peral, J., Gil, D., Medina, J.: Data mining and machine learning techniques for early detection in autism spectrum disorder. Elsevier Inc. (2021). https://doi.org/10.1016/B978-0-12-822822-7.00006-5
8. Goldenberg, S.L., Nir, G., Salcudean, S.E.: A new era: artificial intelligence and machine learning in prostate cancer. Nat. Rev. Urol. **16**, 391–403 (2019). https://doi.org/10.1038/s41585-019-0193-3
9. Mao, A., Omair Shafiq, M.: On the analysis of a public dataset for diabetes. In: 2018 13th International Conference Digital Information Management ICDIM 2018, pp. 88–93 (2018). https://doi.org/10.1109/ICDIM.2018.8847123
10. Concannon, D., Herbst, K., Manley, E.: Developing a data dashboard framework for population health surveillance: widening access to clinical trial findings. JMIR Form. Res. **3**, (2019). https://doi.org/10.2196/11342
11. Xu, X., Ma, J., Huang, X., Luo, X.: Prediction of diabetes with its symptoms based on machine learngin. In: IEEE International Conference on Computer Science, Artificial Intelligence and Electronic Engineering (CSAIEE) (2021)
12. Lopes, M.C., Amorim, M.M., Freitas, V.S., Calumby, R.T.: Survival prediction for oral cancer patients: a machine learning approach. In: Symposium on Knowledge Discovery, Mining and Learning, KDMILE 2021, pp. 97–104 (2021). https://doi.org/10.5753/kdmile.2021.17466
13. Teixeira, F., Zeni, J.L., da Costa, C.A., da Rosa, R.: An analysis of machine learning classifiers in breast cancer diagnosis. In: XLV Latin American Computing Conference (CLEI) (2019)
14. Haucanes, C., Suárez, A.: Aplicación de técnicas de visualización de datos para la inteligencia de negocios (2015)

Blockchain Trends in Education:
A Scientometric Review

Jhon Wilder Sánchez-Obando[1]([⊠]) [iD] and Néstor Darío Duque-Méndez[2] [iD]

[1] Facultad de Ciencias Contables Económicas y Administrativas, Universidad de Manizales, Manizales, Colombia
jwsanchez@umanizales.edu.co

[2] Facultad de Administración, Universidad Nacional de Colombia, Grupo de Ambientes Inteligentes y Adaptativos GAIA, Bogotá, Colombia

Abstract. The rapid development of blockchain technology has influenced various fields, such as financial, healthcare, and supply chain systems. Recently, this technology has also made inroads in education thanks to its unique features, such as decentralization, reliability, and security. Despite the positive side of blockchain, there are some trends of its application to education that require overcoming some problems, such as legal, immutability, and scalability issues. Therefore, a study on blockchain trends in education is considered necessary. This article is a scientometric review of the literature on blockchain trends in education. For this purpose, the results are classified according to 4 identified trends. In this article, we focus on two main topics: educational applications and works by the academic community. The Tree of Science (ToS) method combined with an analysis in VOS viewer is used to subsequently analyze the results in the form of graphs and co-citation networks. In total 1202 papers published between 2016 and 2021 in the Web of Science, Science Direct, IEEE, and Scopus databases were involved in the study, where the ToS algorithm was subsequently applied to identify the most relevant literature on the topic. The results showed that blockchain technology in education presents four trends: educational technology, IEEE and computational blockchain, IEEE and common internet, and finally blockchain management and literacy as a tool to validate information. Finally, it describes some research gaps that need to be addressed.

Keywords: Blockchain in education · Scientometric review · Blockchain applications · Trends blockchain

1 Introduction

Blockchain as a technology has been of growing interest to the scientific community, however, as mentioned by [1], there is a procedure for research in blockchain, which establishes conceptual, descriptive, and predictive levels. Therefore, it is necessary to investigate the contributions of knowledge to the different levels of research in blockchain with which it is possible to support the research problem from the informal and formal logic for the understanding of the reality of the phenomenon under study.

V. Agredo-Delgado et al. (Eds.): CCC 2022, CCIS 1775, pp. 28–43, 2023.
https://doi.org/10.1007/978-3-031-36357-3_3

[2], was the first person to introduce a cryptocurrency which he called: Bitcoin, and with this the blockchain technology. This made it possible to decentralize person-to-person economic transactions without the intermediation of a third party such as banks. To add a new block to the existing blockchain, it is necessary to record transactions and solve a cryptographic equation with high computational demand to reach a consensus in the blockchain. From there, various platforms for blockchain development have emerged, such as Ethereum [3] and Hyper ledger Fabric [4]. Which unlike Bitcoin can work with smart contracts, which emerge as a proposal for the solution of problems in different sectors such as education [5]. Smart contracts are self-executing codes on blockchain to execute peer-to-peer agreement actions without any supervision [3].

Currently, the provision of educational service is provided by educational institutions. Although the educational system offers: access, coverage, permanence, quality, and knowledge, it is not flexible in terms of time and money constraints [6]. In this context, the scientific community has invited the creation of an educational network based on blockchain technology. Thus, [7] indicate that, although the blockchain in education is still in early development, it has the potential to facilitate the reengineering of educational institutions.

[7], manifests areas of blockchain technology research in education as:

- Decentralization: Decentralized and distributed peer-to-peer blockchain architecture implies the elimination of central controlling authority.
- Immutability: data stored in the blockchain are immutable records whose states cannot be modified after their creation. Immutability is related to security, resilience, and irreversibility.
- Transparency: With blockchain technology, it is possible to verify that the data of a transaction has existed at a given time.
- Trust: Blockchain technology shifts trust from the need to trust a centralized authority to the need to trust the technology itself.

The Blockchain is a technology that stands out because it allows transparency, integrity, and traceability of data to authenticate information and therefore reduces transaction costs and improves the efficiency of public services [8]. On the other hand, [9] consider that the Blockchain is a disruptive technology that allows transactions in a decentralized manner, so the government loses its purpose of Primus Inter Pares in the public sector since a centralized authority is no longer necessary to govern, control or reduce risks in the provision of public services or implementation of public policies [10].

According to [11], there are challenges in various sectors such as education, where it is not clear how to initiate a process of implementation of the technologies of the fourth industrial revolution 4RI, so it is necessary to join efforts in research concerning the construction of frameworks for the implementation of the technologies of the fourth industrial revolution 4RI in education [12].

A field in growing interest is the application of Blockchain in education, in a special way applied to individual, group, and national institutions to offload some applications such as inventory management, student records, and distribution of public funds [13].

This article is organized as follows. Section 2 presents the scientometric review procedure adopted in this study. Section 3 shows the results of the review scientometric. Section 4 provides an in-depth analysis and discussion of the results obtained. Based on the results of the review, Sect. 5 identifies knowledge gaps. Section 6 presents the conclusions of the study.

2   Research Methodology

The search methodology proposed by [14], allows for a systematic literature review that explores the relationship between blockchain and education. The results show future research trends for blockchain technology in education. The systematic literature review was constructed based on the protocol established by [15]. The use of the above methodology is chosen because of the rigor and clarity in the stages of the methodological design appropriate for the present study.

2.1   Definition of Research Question

This step consists of establishing the questions guiding the research to obtain a detailed vision of the topic addressed. The objectives of the research are i) to discover blockchain and education trends ii) to classify blockchain and education research iii) to identify blockchain and education research cooperation networks and iv) to analyze blockchain and education trends research opportunities. Table 1 shows the search equations.

Table 1. Research question

Resarch question	Aims
RQ1: ¿ Where and when were research topics on blockchain for education published?	Find research areas, as well as their publications, publication times, and whether the research areas are relevant to the scientific community
RQ2: ¿What areas of blockchain research and education exist?	Understand the current state of blockchain technology in education
RQ3: ¿What is the Tree of Science of blockchain and education?	Illustrate collaboration and co-citation networks between countries and authors in blockchain and education
RQ4: ¿What are the trends in blockchain and education publications?	Find the cloud words of research trends reported in publications for blockchain and education

2.2 Search

This stage consists of collecting articles from the following databases: Scopus, Web of Science (WoS), Science direct, and IEEE. This selection of databases is due to the tolerance that the ToS algorithm has for the joint work between the Scopus and WoS databases, therefore, the Science Direct database is included to deepen the search results, since the results are broader than the previous databases. The IEEE database is also included since it deals with technology such as a blockchain, this specialized database would yield important studies on its implementation in education. The Google Scholar database is not included because the present study focuses on the use of the ToS tool and not on the Publish or Perish software in the PRISMA protocol. The search was conducted in April 2022. To search the articles, the search equation: blockchain and education was used. Table 2 presents the structure of the search equations for each database.

Table 2. Searches in database

Scientific database	Query strings
Scopus	TITLE-ABS-KEY ("blockchain" AND "education")
Web of Science (WoS)	"blockchain" AND "education"
Science Direct	"blockchain" AND "education"
IEEE	"blockchain" AND "education"

At the end of this stage 180 articles, as shown in Fig. 1 shows the classification procedure of the articles found to which exclusion criteria are applied and Fig. 1 shows the annual production from 2016 to 2021 in the 4 databases (Fig. 2).

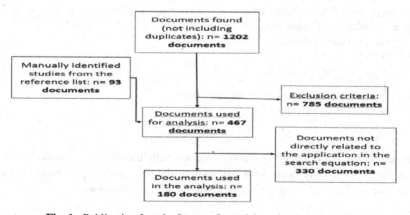

Fig. 1. Publication founds. Source: Own elaboration based on [14].

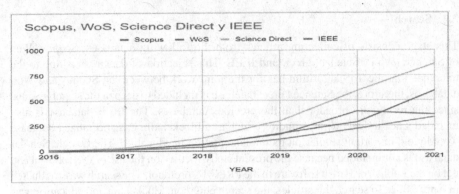

Fig. 2. Annual production. Source: Own elaboration.

2.3 Study Selection

This step consists of choosing the relevant papers that would help answer the research questions. To do so, a set of inclusion and exclusion criteria are defined in Table 3.

Table 3. Inclusion and exclusion criteria for relevant documents

Inclusion criteria	Exclusion criteria
Documents demonstrating the application of blockchain in education that are part of the grey literature	Editorial Comments and Opinions
Papers proposing feasible solutions to blockchain problems in education (method, technique, model, and conceptual framework)	Documents that present surveys
Papers proposing solutions that have been evaluated (implemented, simulated, and mathematically modeled) that are part of the grey literature	Documents written in languages other than English
Documents produced in English only	
Papers published in journals and conferences that are part of the grey literature	Books

Based on the above results, we proceeded to exclude documents outside the scope of this study. Thus, only documents that met all the inclusion criteria were included, filtering the studies according to the title, abstract, and list of keywords.

2.4 Data Extraction

This stage consists of gathering the information necessary to address the research questions of this study. Therefore, we established the review criteria that contained 9 review criteria, implemented in 180 documents included in this scientometric review as shown in Table 4.

Table 4. Criteria for reviewing documents

Criteria	Description
Name of Authors	Identity of the authors of the publication
Title	Name of publication
DOI	Code for your respective search
Affiliation	University and affiliation department
Abstract	Report, type of research, methodology, and results
Keywords	Indication of the areas of research for publication
Type of Document	Article, conference, book chapter, and book
Language	English or Spanish
Source	databases: Scopus, Web of Science, IEEE y Science Direct

3   Results of Scientometric Review

We proceed to analyze the 180 articles through a network analysis in the construction of the science tree supported by the VOS viewer platform to answer each of the research questions. The initial search on the search equation defined in the systematic literature review was carried out on Web of Science, Scopus, Science direct, and IEEE.

The results were exported to the ToS scientometric platform that generates a tree structure, in its root are located the classic articles, in the trunk the structural documents and in the leaves, the recent documents, in this way subcategories are determined by citation analysis. Co-citation analysis is a recognized technique for identifying different areas of a research topic.

The first 500 documents of the search result are exported to a file in txt format, and so on until 1202 documents are found, which will be the seed of the tree of science for the bibliographic analysis process, using an algorithm based on graphs.

The data in the seed corresponding to the name of the authors, name of the journal, journal edition, abstract, keywords, affiliation, country of origin, DOI, and the references cited in each article; these data allow classifying the results to establish a category analogous to one of the parts of a tree (root, trunk, and leaves).

The.txt file is loaded into the R Studio Cloud software, a new project is generated and the ToS algorithm is installed, which generates a graph that is composed of nodes and edges, in which the articles or research papers are the nodes and the connections between them are the edges.

And articles that cite others in the network (root and trunk) but are not cited, will be leaves [16] and [17]. In the results delivered by ToS, the seminal works of the field of study should appear, which extends the temporary analysis initially defined in the search. This situation is generated by the graph analysis algorithms on which the ToS tool is based and by the inclusion of co-citations to generate the tree [18].

The perspectives of blockchain, education, and public budget, are constructed by citation analysis, through a clustering algorithm [19], then the concepts that compose each perspective are identified and analyzed from text mining of the R Cloud package.

It is observed that the network has 8001 nodes and 15312 links (references between articles), this graph is the product of the web scraping algorithm that generates a file in R.

3.1 RQ1: ¿Where and when were Research Topics on Blockchain for Education Published?

To answer this question, we proceeded to identify the research areas of blockchain and education through the VOS viewer platform where the 180 documents found in the 4 databases consulted were used, as shown in Fig. 3.

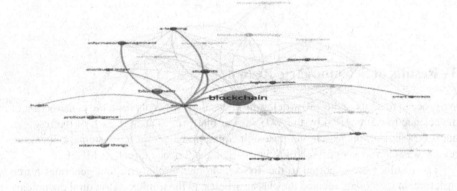

Fig. 3. Topic research of blockchain and education. Source: Own elaboration in VOS viewer.

From Fig. 3, it can be observed how the complete search equation presents a less complex network with 4 clusters identified: green, red, blue, and yellow.

- Green cluster: is the cluster that shows a direct relationship between blockchain and education with the types of blockchain as public or decentralized and the type of computational method it uses for public fund management purposes.
- Red cluster: is the cluster that shows the relationship of students and learning management, this indicates that for the complete search equation pedagogical and didactic applications are developed.
- Yellow cluster: is the cluster that shows the solution in the implementation of blockchain in educational public funds, from the hybridization with other technologies such as the internet of things (IoT) and artificial intelligence (AI).
- Blue cluster: is the cluster that shows the emergence of different technologies that develop cryptocurrencies such as bitcoin, as a solution for the management of public funds in education.

3.2 RQ2: ¿What Areas of Blockchain Research and Education Exist?

This question is answered by classifying the 180 articles found in the different research topics, problems in education where blockchain technology has been implemented and the countries where the publications or research is performed in the period 2016 to 2021 as shown in Fig. 4.

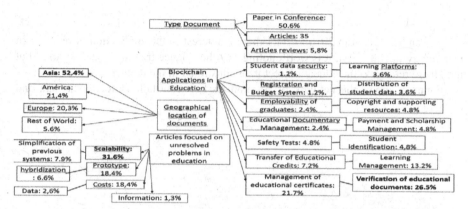

Fig. 4. Classification of documents reviewed. Source: Own elaboration based on ToS and VOS viewer.

From the figure above it is observed that most of the articles found are articles published in conferences with 50.6%, concerning the applications of blockchain technology in education most of them are focused on the verification of student documents such as diplomas and transcripts with 26.5%.

The geographical location where most articles are published concerning blockchain and education is Asia with 52.4% focused on the countries of China, India, and South Korea respectively, finally, the published articles have focused on the problem of scalability of blockchain technology with 31.6%.

The previous figure fulfills the function of illustrating through a diagram the results of the scientometric review, which shows the percentages of research participation in specific problems of technology in the field of education. This allows contrasting with the trends reported in the results.

3.3 RQ3: ¿What is the Tree of Science of Blockchain and Education?

The tree of science that was found consists of 275 documents in total classified in ToS as follows: 10 documents are root documents i.e. they are classical documents that due to their high citation score transforms them into a classical document, and 205 trunk documents known as structural documents that cite root documents but these, in turn, are cited by newer documents, finally 60 leaf documents that cite trunk documents and root documents but are not cited by other authors. Table 5 shows the main root, trunk, and leaf documents classified by their level of citation and by their year of publication.

Table 5. Structure of Tree of Science for blockchain and education

Part of Tree	Authors
Root (5)	[2, 20–22] and [7]
Trunk (5)	[23–26] and [27]
Leaves (2)	[28] and [29]

As can be seen from 2016 to 2021 there is interest in the application of blockchain technology in education, it is worth noting that the science tree found 275 articles, but not all are related to the education sector, as illustrated in the table above.

Figure 5 shows the network of co-citations between authors for blockchain and education.

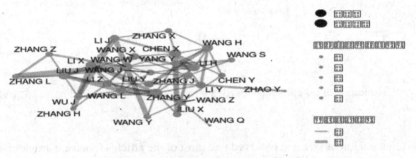

Fig. 5. Network co-citation of Authors. Source: Own elaboration based in ToS.

From Fig. 5, it can be observed how the complete search equation presents a less complex network with 5 clusters identified in: green, red, blue, purple, and yellow. This network is characterized by not being an extensive and dense network in the process of research and co-citation of authors during blockchain and education research.

- Green cluster: 6 authors of Asian origin are observed in this cluster.
- Red cluster: 6 authors of Asian origin are observed in this cluster.
- Yellow cluster: 6 authors of Asian origin are observed in this cluster.
- Blue cluster: 5 authors of Asian origin are observed in this cluster.
- Purple cluster: 4 authors of Asian origin are observed in this cluster.

As shown in Fig. 5, the scientometric algorithm highlighted Asian authors, since they represent the largest number of published documents as defined in Fig. 4, since more than 52.4% of world production corresponds to the continent of Asia. Similarly, the author co-citation network highlights the relationship between the authors about the thematic area of this study, therefore, the result of Fig. 5 is explained.

Figure 6 shows the network of co-occurrence of keywords for blockchain and education.

From Fig. 6, it can be observed how the complete search equation presents a more complex network with 4 clusters identified in: green, red, purple, and blue. This network

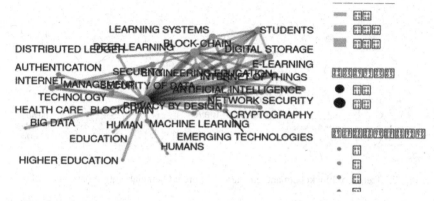

Fig. 6. Network co-occurrence of keywords. Source: Own elaboration based in ToS.

is characterized by being an extensive and dense network in the process of research and the co-occurrence of keywords during blockchain and education research.

- Green cluster: This cluster includes technologies related to the blockchain to be implemented in the solution of different problems in education, a total of 9 technologies ranging from artificial intelligence, internet of things to cryptography.
- Red cluster: This cluster shows the different fields and problems where blockchain technology is implemented, with a total of 10 applications, including privacy, authentication, preventive health, and security management.
- Purple cluster: This is the smallest cluster, keywords such as emerging human technologies and machine learning are observed, in total only 2 keywords are observed.
- Blue cluster: In this cluster, we observe the specific applications of blockchain in education, in total 9 scenarios of blockchain application in education are observed, among which we highlight learning systems, digital stages, and deep learning.

3.4   RQ4: ¿What are the Trends in Blockchain and Education?

Figure 7 shows the keywords of the most representative trends or clusters for blockchain and education.

From the previous figure, the trends found as a result of the ToS algorithm can be observed, therefore, we proceed to describe each of the four clusters found.

- *Trend 1*: In this cluster are the documents related to the identification of blockchain applications in solving education problems, in which the root of the tree in this cluster is [30], who developed a system for transferring educational credits between higher education institutions and companies in order to guarantee the skills of the new employee. On the other hand, the trunk considered as a structural document of the solutions proposed by blockchain in education is [31], who establishes a taxonomy for blockchain that addresses different problematics in education. And as a leaf, we have [32], who proposes a blockchain model for the payment of courses located in MOOCs of educational institutions. A total of 185 articles were found in this cluster related to blockchain and education. For this trend, the algorithm found 2919 documents.

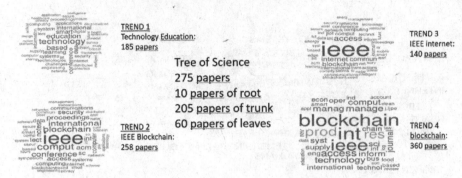

Fig. 7. Trends of blockchain and education. Source: Own elaboration based in ToS.

- *Trend 2*: This includes documents related to the development of the blockchain from the IEEE, with a focus on security in which the root of the tree of this cluster is [2], who first developed the structure of the blockchain chain that made possible economic transfers without intermediaries with the bitcoin cryptocurrency. On the other hand, the trunk considered as a structural document in the development of blockchain technology is [33], who proposed the structure of smart contracts or Smart Contract to ensure the security of transactions in public and decentralized blockchain networks. And as a leaf we have [34], who proposes a new elliptic curve algorithm for the proof of stagnation and work of a public network known as Gamal cryptographic and encryption algorithm. A total of 258 items were found in this cluster related to blockchain and education. For this trend, the algorithm found 1772 documents.
- *Trend 3*: In this are the documents related to the dissemination of technology on the internet from the IEEE, in which the root of this cluster is [35], who proposes different issues related to the security of data of higher education students focusing its effort on the traceability of degree certificates. On the other hand, the trunk considered as a structural document in the certification of student documents is [36], who proposes a decentralized blockchain network assisted by smart contracts and virtual wallet for the traceability and tracking of degree certificates by the ministry of education and employing companies. [37], establishes a public and private blockchain network structure for various applications focused on solving problems of identity and data security of higher education students. A total of 140 articles related to blockchain and education were found in this cluster. For this trend the algorithm found 1531 documents.
- *Trend 4*: In this are the documents related to reliable storage of academic records, in which the root of this cluster is [38], who proposes through a systematic literature review solution of blockchain technology in different sectors. On the other hand, the trunk considered as a structural document in the use of blockchain technology in the development of cryptocurrencies is [39], who proposes a decentralized blockchain network for various applications through the use of cryptocurrencies. And as a leaf, we have [40], who establishes a decentralized application based on smart contracts for sharing prevention or health care data of patients of a health prevention system,

which guarantees the privacy and security of patient data. A total of 360 items were found in this cluster. For this cluster, the algorithm found 1238 documents.

Figure 8 shows the trends in blockchain research and education resulting from the scientometric literature review.

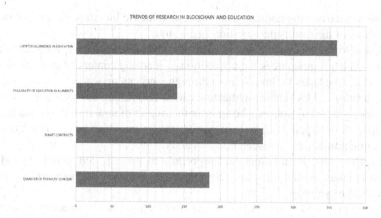

Fig. 8. Trends of research in blockchain and education. Source: Own elaboration based in ToS.

From the figure above, it is observed that of the four trends found by the scientometric review there is a greater number of papers published on cryptocurrencies in education, thus the implementation of cryptocurrencies for the solution of various problems in education becomes an area of interest to the academic community.

Figure 9 shows the thematic map of blockchain research and education resulting from the scientometric literature review.

Fig. 9. Trends of research in blockchain and education. Source: Own elaboration based in Bibliometrix.

Based on the figure above, a Cartesian plane is observed between the degree of development and the degree of relevance that divides the plane into four quadrants which are motor themes, basic themes, emergence of themes due to the decline of other themes and niche themes. In which it is observed that the highest degree of development are the niche topics that are growing as internet and management systems, as well as emerging topic in research is technology.

4 Discussion

This section discusses the findings from the scientometric literature review. we proceed to an analysis of the results per question in the study.

[32], develops a blockchain architecture that gives rise to the cryptocurrency called Edu Coin, which it guarantees the acquisition of learning content of courses stored in MOOCs (Massive Open Online Course) through a private network.

[41], develops a blockchain architecture called TEduChain that guarantees the tracking of money granted by donors who sponsor the studies of underprivileged students, for their support through scholarships in higher education, for which he uses smart contracts for economic transactions between scholars and donor.

BCDiploma [40], is an influential European start-up that "dematerializes and automates the issuance of diplomas and certificates". Its solution has been widely used by universities across Europe.

[42] have proposed a blockchain-based system that evaluates students' professional capabilities based on their academic achievements and performances. The assessment value of students' abilities not only depends on the grade of the school course but also includes academic achievements and off-campus internships [42].

5 Research Gap

Finally, based on [43], it is necessary that for future research the blockchain and education trends found to allow to leave the technological paradigm that the specialized academic community has focused its efforts on solving the problems of technological scalability of the blockchain and allow other academic communities from the social to conduct research against the thinking and social appropriation of technology in sectors that are considered social constructs such as education.

6 Conclusions

The blockchain and education relationship is relatively new, emerging in mid-2016 as a response to the manifest need to present blockchain-based solution alternatives to different problems in the education sector, and thanks to the scientific works published, it has been possible to build definitions and concepts of blockchain and education, which allow a contribution to technological initiatives in the education sector, with special emphasis on higher education.

Four blockchain and education trends were found, the first one analyzes blockchain technology in education, and the second one shows the importance for the educational community to research on blockchain in education focusing on the technological scalability problems to implement the technology in education published in IEEE journal classified in Q1, the third one evidences the interest of the academic community to visualize their technical contributions in the IEEE and the fourth one exposes blockchain and its relationship with other sectors or areas of knowledge.

As future research, it is suggested to use other literature review protocols such as PRISMA with a greater number of databases including that of google scholar and the use of Publish or Perish software.

Declaration

Competing interests: The authors declare that they have no conflict of interest.

References

1. Zhao, J.L., Fan, S., Yan, J.: Overview of business innovations and research opportunities in blockchain and introduction to the special issue. Fin. Innov. **2**(1), 1–7 (2016). https://doi.org/10.1186/s40854-016-0049-2
2. Nakamoto, S.: Bitcoin: A peer-to-peer electronic cash system. Decentralized Bus. Rev., p. 21260 (2008)
3. Buterin, V.: A next-generation smart contract and decentralized application platform. white Pap. **3**(37), 1–2 (2014)
4. Androulaki, E., et al.: Hyperledger fabric: a distributed operating system for permissioned blockchains. In: Proceedings of the Thirteenth EuroSys Conference, pp. 1–15 (2018)
5. Yasin, A., Liu, L.: An online identity and smart contract management system. In: 2016 IEEE 40th Annual Computer Software and Applications Conference (COMPSAC), **2**, pp. 192–198 (2016)
6. Choi, T.-M.: Financing Product Development Projects in the Blockchain Era: Initial Coin Offerings Versus Traditional Bank Loans. IEEE Trans. Eng. Manag., pp. 1–13 (2020). https://doi.org/10.1109/TEM.2020.3032426
7. Grech, A., Camilleri, A.F.: Blockchain in Education. Publications Office of the European Union, Luxembourg (2017)
8. Beck, R., Stenum Czepluch, J., Lollike, N., Malone, S.: Blockchain–the Gateway to Trust-Free Cryptographic Transactions (2016)
9. Pierre, J., Peters, B.G.: Governing complex societies: Trajectories and scenarios. Gov. Complex Soc. Trajectories Scenar., pp. 1–158 (2005). https://doi.org/10.1057/9780230512641
10. Miscione, G., Ziolkowski, R., Zavolokina, L., Schwabe, G.: Tribal Governance: The Business of Blockchain Authentication. Accessed: 05 Nov 2021. http://hdl.handle.net/10125/50455
11. Deloitte Insights. La cuarta revolución industrial está aquí - ¿ está usted preparado. Deloitte Touche Ltda (2018)
12. Kapur, R.: Problems and Issues in Teacher Education and Curriculum Development (2018)
13. Albeanu, G.: Blockchain technology and education. In: The 12th International Conference on Virtual Learning ICVL, pp. 271–275 (2017)
14. Bartels, E.M.: How to perform a systematic search. Best Pract. Res. Clin. Rheumatol. **27**(2), 295–306 (2013). https://doi.org/10.1016/j.berh.2013.02.001
15. Vivares, J.A., Avella, L., Sarache, W.: Trends and Challenges in Operations Strategy Research: Findings from a Systematic Literature Review (2022)
16. Zuluaga, M., Robledo, S., Osorio Zuluaga, G.A., Yathe, L., Gonzalez, D., Taborda, G.: Metabolómica y Pesticidas: Revisión sistemática de literatura usando teoría de grafos para el análisis de referencias. Nova (2016). https://doi.org/10.22490/24629448.1735

17. Robledo-Giraldo, S., Duque-Méndez, N.D., Zuluaga-Giraldo, J.I.: Difusión de productos a través de redes sociales: una revisión bibliográfica utilizando la teoría de grafos. Respuestas (2013). https://doi.org/10.22463/0122820x.361

18. Zuluaga, M., Arbelaez-Echeverri, O., Robledo, S., Osorio-Zuluaga, G.A., Duque-Méndez, N.: Tree of Science - ToS: A Web-Based Tool for Scientific Literature Recommendation. Search Less, Research More!. Issues Sci. Technol. Librariansh. **2022**(100) (2022). https://doi.org/10.29173/ISTL2696

19. Blondel, V.D., Guillaume, J.L., Hendrickx, J.M., De Kerchove, C., Lambiotte, R.: Local leaders in random networks. Phys. Rev. E - Stat. Nonlinear, Soft Matter Phys. (2008). https://doi.org/10.1103/PhysRevE.77.036114

20. Özyilmaz, K.R., Yurdakul, A.: Work-in-progress: integrating low-power iot devices to a blockchain-based infrastructure. In: Proc. Int. Conf. Embedded Softw.(EMSOFT), pp. 1–2 (2017)

21. Chen, G., Xu, B., Lu, M., Chen, N.-S.: Exploring blockchain technology and its potential applications for education. Smart Learning Environ. **5**(1), 1 (2018). https://doi.org/10.1186/s40561-017-0050-x

22. Sharples, M., Domingue, J.: The blockchain and kudos: a distributed system for educational record, reputation and reward. In: Verbert, K., Sharples, M., Klobučar, T. (eds.) EC-TEL 2016. LNCS, vol. 9891, pp. 490–496. Springer, Cham (2016). https://doi.org/10.1007/978-3-319-45153-4_48

23. Delgado-von-Eitzen, C., Anido-Rifón, L., Fernández-Iglesias, M.J.: Blockchain applications in education: a systematic literature review. Appl. Sci. **11**(24), 11811 (2021)

24. Lam, T.Y., Dongol, B.: A blockchain-enabled e-learning platform. Interact. Learn. Environ., pp. 1–23 (2020)

25. Lizcano, D., Lara, J.A., White, B., Aljawarneh, S.: Blockchain-based approach to create a model of trust in open and ubiquitous higher education. J. Comput. High. Educ. **32**(1), 109–134 (2019). https://doi.org/10.1007/s12528-019-09209-y

26. Alammary, A., Alhazmi, S., Almasri, M., Gillani, S.: Blockchain-based applications in education: a systematic review. Appl. Sci. **9**(12), 2400 (2019)

27. Wanotayapitak, S., Saraubon, K., Nilsook, P.: Process design of cooperative education management system by cloud-based blockchain e-portfolio.. Int. J. Online Biomed. Eng. **15**(8) (2019)

28. Babu, E.S., Srinivasarao, B.K.N., Kavati, I., Rao, M.S.: Verifiable authentication and issuance of academic certificates using permissioned blockchain network. Int. J. Inf. Secur. Priv. **16**(1), 1–24 (2022)

29. Chaiyarak, S., Koednet, A., Nilsook, P.: Blockchain, IoT and fog computing for smart education management. Int. J. Educ. Inf. Technol. **14**(1), 52–61 (2020)

30. Turkanović, M., Hölbl, M., Košič, K., Heričko, M., Kamišalić, A.: EduCTX: a blockchain-based higher education credit platform. IEEE Access **6**, 5112–5127 (2018). https://doi.org/10.1109/ACCESS.2018.2789929

31. Singh, S.K., Jenamani, M., Dasgupta, D., Das, S.: A conceptual model for Indian public distribution system using consortium blockchain with on-chain and off-chain trusted data. Inf. Technol. Dev. **27**(3), 499–523 (2021). https://doi.org/10.1080/02681102.2020.1847024

32. Lu, L., et al.: EduCoin: a secure and efficient payment solution for MOOC environment. In: 2019 IEEE International Conference on Blockchain (Blockchain), (2019). Accessed: 04 June 2022. https://ieeexplore-ieee-org.ezproxy.unal.edu.co/document/8946233/

33. Szabo, N.: Formalizing and securing relationships on public networks. First monday (1997)

34. Nouman, M., Ullah, K., Azam, M.: Secure digital transactions in the education sector using blockchain. EAI Endorsed Trans. Scalable Inf. Syst. **9**(35) (2022). https://doi.org/10.4108/EAI.3-11-2021.171758

35. Zheng, Z., Xie, S., Dai, H., Chen, X., Wang, H.: An overview of blockchain technology: architecture, consensus, and future trends. In: 2017 IEEE International Congress on Big Data (BigData Congress), pp. 557–564 (2017)

36. Alnafrah, I., Mouselli, S.: Revitalizing blockchain technology potentials for smooth academic records management and verification in low-income countries. Int. J. Educ. Dev. **85** (2021). https://doi.org/10.1016/j.ijedudev.2021.102460

37. Jayne Fleener, M.: Blockchain technologies: a study of the future of education. J. High. Educ. Theory Pract. **22**(1), pp. 26–45 (2022). https://doi.org/10.33423/JHETP.V22I1.4956

38. Sultan, K., Ruhi, U., Lakhani, R.: Conceptualizing Blockchains: Characteristics & Applications (2018). arXiv Prepr. arXiv1806.03693

39. Kraft, D.: Difficulty control for blockchain-based consensus systems. Peer-to-Peer Networking Appl. **9**(2), 397–413 (2015)

40. Wang, C., Shen, J., Lai, J.-F., Liu, J.: B-TSCA: blockchain assisted trustworthiness scalable computation for V2I authentication in VANETs. IEEE Trans. Emerg. Top. Comput. **9**(3), 1386–1396 (2020)

41. Rashid, M.A., Deo, K., Prasad, D., Singh, K., Chand, S., Assaf, M.: TEduChain: a blockchain-based platform for crowdfunding tertiary education. Knowl. Eng. Rev. **35**, e27 (2020). https://doi.org/10.1017/S0269888920000326

42. Zhao, S., Li, S., Yao, Y.: Blockchain enabled industrial internet of things technology. IEEE Trans. Comput. Soc. Syst. **6**(6), 1442–1453 (2019)

43. Jover, J.: LA CIENCIA Y LA TECNOLOGIA COMO PROCESOS SOCIALES. Lo que la educación científica no debería olvidar (2018)

Comparison of Deployment Options for Microservices in the Cloud

Daniela Beltran[(✉)] and Mariela Curiel

Pontificia Universidad Javeriana, Bogotá, Colombia
{d_beltran,mcuriel}@javeriana.edu.co

Abstract. In the context of digital transformation, organizations must change their systems and technology platforms. Cloud Computing is a powerful technology available at disposal of organizations to accelerate transformation plans. The cloud offers several benefits such as greater agility in development, quick and easy access to information from anywhere and anytime, as well as great savings since you pay for what you use, thus reducing infrastructure investment costs. Another great advantage is that cloud providers offer many options to migrate services and applications. In this sense, it is important to characterize the resource and pattern usage of applications to choose the cloud service that offers the best relation cost/benefit. In this article, we focus on microservices and analyze three options for deploying them in the Google Cloud Platform: virtual machines (Compute Engine), Google Kubernetes Engine and Cloud Functions. Once the services are deployed, we generate artificial load to measure the response times and the number of requirements served. We also calculate the cost of the three options. The results agree with other studies that recommend serverless options such as Cloud Functions over container-based options or virtual machines. While these studies focus primarily on performance and cost, our work also addresses elements related to ease of deployment.

Keywords: Microservices · Containers · Serverless Functions

1 Introduction

Businesses today are looking for technologies that accelerate digital transformation. Digital transformation refers to use modern digital technologies to create or modify business processes, culture, and customer experiences to adapt changing business and market dynamics. One of these digital technologies is **Cloud Computing** because of its various advantages: it offers high availability, scalability, and the option of to pay only for what you use. Another important feature of cloud computing is agility, as the time to develop and deploy applications is significantly reduced.

The adoption of cloud computing leads organizations to start migrating or refactoring their monolith-based applications to microservices architecture. Microservices are a set

---

The authors of the article would like to thank the Google staff for the academic account that allowed us to perform these tests.

V. Agredo-Delgado et al. (Eds.): CCC 2022, CCIS 1775, pp. 44–57, 2023.
https://doi.org/10.1007/978-3-031-36357-3_4

of smaller, loosely coupled components that can be developed, tested, deployed, scaled, operated, and upgraded independently.

Cloud providers provide a variety of computing services for the deployment of microservices. These services have different characteristics in terms of performance, cost, ease of deployment and control over the infrastructure. Options that are suitable for deploying microservices in the cloud include virtual machines, container-based services and serverless options.

This paper presents a comparison of the deployment and execution of a microservices benchmark (*Sock Shop*) [1] on three services from Google Cloud Platform: Google Compute Engine, Google Kubernetes Engine and Google Functions.

The results show that the use of Kubernetes offers better throughput and response times compared to the performance of benchmark components on virtual machines. Additionally, the result of Cloud Functions outperforms the previous options as response times tend to be constant regardless of the large volume of requests made.

This document is structured as follows: in the Sect. 2, the definitions related to the research are presented. Then we discuss some related work in the Sect. 3. The Sect. 4 describes the benchmark and the different deployment options in the cloud. Experiments and results are presented in the Sect. 5. Finally, we conclude in Sect. 6.

2 Background

2.1 Microservices

The microservices architectural style is an approach to developing a single application as a set of small services, each running in its own process and communicating with lightweight mechanisms such as HTTP, RESTful web services, message queues, etc. This model facilitates the design of software architectures that should be flexible, modular, and easy to evolve [2]. Their main characteristics include: a) microservices can be developed in different programming languages and by different teams; b) they are independently deployable and at execution time, each microservice can scale independently according to its workload; c) microservices provide access to their logic and data through a well-defined network interface; d) they are highly maintainable, testable and their loosely coupled design makes them more fault tolerant as the failure of one service will not affect the entire system [3].

2.2 Virtual Machines

Virtualize in computing refers to the abstraction of some physical component into a logical object. Gerald J. Popek and Robert P. Goldberg, in their 1974 paper "Formal Requirements for Virtualizable Third Generation Architectures describe the functions and properties of virtual machines and virtual machine monitors (VMM) that we still use today. According to Popek and Goldberg's definition, a virtual machine (VM) can virtualize all hardware resources, including processors, memory, storage, and network connectivity. A virtual machine monitor (VMM), or hypervisor, is the software that provides the environment in which VMs operate. In this paper, we will be using Google Compute Engine (**CE**) which is the secure and customizable computing service that allows virtual machines to be created and run on Google's infrastructure.

2.3 Containers

Virtualization at the operating system (OS) level allows for the creation of multiple iso-lated user space instances, called in different ways such as containers (LXC, Solaris containers, Docker, Podman), zones (Solaris containers), virtual private servers (OpenVZ), partitions, virtual environments, jails (FreeBSD jail), etc. In this article, we will adopt the name of containers.

In the virtualization at the OS level, containers share the kernel and hardware of the host operating system. The host operating system implements several measures to increase the degree of separation it maintains between processes, thereby creating this notion of containers or contexts. Programs running inside of a container can only see the container's contents and devices assigned to the container. Because the operating system is shared, container images are lighter than those of virtual machines are.

One of the most widely used technologies for application containerization is Docker [4], which increases productivity and reduces costs, allowing any developer, in any environment, to develop robust applications. Docker containers wrap a piece of software in a file system that contains everything needed to run it (code, runtime, system tools, system libraries and settings.), ensuring that it will always run the same way, regardless of its deployment environment [5].

With the rise of microservices, it is very likely that the hosting, deployment, and management of thousands of services will be required. The use of containers will help in this address by separating applications from infrastructure dependencies.

2.4 Container Orchestration

Managing a few containers is not the same as managing hundreds or thousands at production scales. Container orchestration automates the deployment, management, scaling, and networking of containers. Container orchestration can be used in any environment where containers are used. Some examples of container orchestration tools are Kubernetes, Mesos + Marathon and Docker Swarm. Kubernetes, also known as K8s [6], is an open-source system for automating the deployment, scaling and management of containerized applications. It is a highly portable orchestration service that can run in the cloud or on clusters hosted in other [7] environments.

Figure 1 shows the Kubernetes architecture. One of the main components is the **master** or "brain" of the container cluster, where the central server is hosted. The master maintains the REST services used, defines the cluster and queries workload status. The role of the **master** is to schedule workloads in the form of **pods** on the cluster nodes. The concept of **Pods** allows containers to be logically grouped together, providing a logical entity that can be replicated, scheduled and whose load can be balanced [8]. Another important element is the **replication controller**, which ensures that the correct number of replicas of a pod are running at any given time. Finally, the **etcd** runs as a backup store for the data. Interactions with Kubernetes are done via the **kubectl** script or REST service calls to the API.

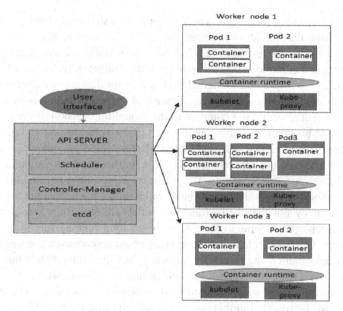

Fig. 1. Kubernetes Architecture

2.5 Serverless Computing

Serverless is a cloud-native development model that makes it possible to design and run applications without the need to manage infrastructure. Serverless computing brings several advantages: a) The programmer does not care about the infrastructure and can therefore focus only on the solution being developed; b) costs are reduced, since only the service execution time is charged for; c) when managed services are used, the service provider automatically provides high availability and auto-scaling [9].

Serverless is not limited to server instances but extends to other areas, too, such as: Serverless databases (e.g. Aurora on AWS), DevOps pipelines, Kubernetes, etc. On the other hand, Function as a Service (FaaS) is a model where the developers create the application logic, and the code is executed in stateless compute instances that are managed by the cloud provider. Serverless functions are triggered by a specific event such as message queues, HTTP requests, etc. Some of the FaaS options currently available include: Azure Functions, AWS Lambda, Google Cloud Functions and Oracle Cloud Functions. In a FaaS model, the client only pays for the function when it is used.

3   Related Work

In this section, we review similar work and highlight the differences with the results presented in this paper.

The authors of [10] compare the costs of a web application developed and deployed using the following approaches: 1) a monolithic architecture, 2) a microservices architecture operated by the cloud client, and 3) a microservices architecture operated by the cloud provider using AWS Lambda. They present a simple case study where only two services from the full set of services offered by the original application are considered. The performance tests allowed them to conclude that the use of microservices can help reduce infrastructure costs by up to 13.42%. Additionally, the use of serverless services such as AWS Lambda, designed exclusively for deploying microservices at a more granular level, allows companies to reduce their infrastructure costs by as much as 77.08%. In our work, we did not compare to the monolithic version of the benchmark, nor did we do an on-premises deployment. Like [10], we present cost and performance considerations. This work was performed on a different cloud provider.

The work described in [11] compares the main options for deploying microservices in the cloud: containers and functions. The performance comparison is made in terms of scalability, reliability, cost, and latency. The research shows that neither the containerized deployment strategy nor the use of functions satisfy all scenarios. For example, the containerized deployment strategy is less costly for long-running services, versus the use of functions. On the other hand, microservices whose responses can be large are more suitable for deployment using FaaS, due to their agility in scaling. While this elasticity of functions allows for a more comfortable handling of peaks in workload, container-based deployment is still more cost-effective when the load is composed of regular traffic patterns. The work presented in this paper was less ambitious since scalability aspects were not evaluated and more reliability-related experiments can be performed as future work.

A final example is the work by [12] that analyzes the performance of container-based virtualization technologies in the cloud. Authors conducted experiments in Docker and Flockport (LXC) using the use of CPU, memory, and I/O devices as performance metrics. The experiments show a low overhead in memory or CPU utilization by Docker or Flockport, while I/O and OS interactions incurred higher overhead. Therefore, applications with higher I/O operations will have more disadvantages when using these technologies.

4   Case Study

The work described in [1] compares three benchmarks Acme Air, Socks Shop and Music Store, in order to choose the most suitable one to represent a microservices application. The comparison evaluates architectural aspects and generalities such as explicit topological view, easy access, continuous integration support, and automatic deployment.

The authors conclude that Socks Shop is a benchmark well documented and implemented following a clear design vision based on some well-known DevOps technologies. Additionally, Sock Shop supports multiple technologies and multiple container orchestration tools. All the above features led us to select Socks Shop in our research to evaluate different cloud services.

Socks Shop [13] simulates the user-facing part of an e-commerce website that sells socks. It was developed using Spring Boot, Go and Node.js, with the specific aim of aiding the demonstration and testing of existing microservice and cloud-native technologies. The benchmark is divided into five components: order management, catalog, payments, users, and shopping cart. It has twenty-two microservices.

For this work we started by selecting the **order management** and **shopping cart** microservices, both developed in Java, under a traditional layered architecture. The **shopping cart** microservice as shown in Fig. 2, is composed of a controller with the operations to add, remove and get the cart items, implemented with the get, put, and post methods of the http protocol. Additionally, it has a repository that oversees communicating with the database in MongoDB.

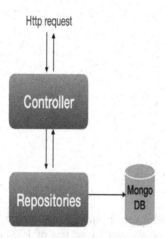

Fig. 2. Shopping Cart Microservice Architecture

The **order management** microservice also has methods to create, delete and get user orders, but it has an asynchronous service as an intermediate layer between the controller and repositories, see Fig. 3.

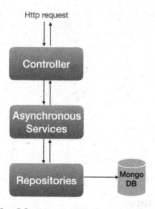

Fig. 3. Order Management Microservice Architecture

4.1 Costs

To analyze the costs of each deployment option, the Google calculator was used. Table 1 shows the services and required parameters for the cost calculation. The load balancer is required for deployment in GKE.

Table 1. Parameters for cost calculation

Service	Type of Machine	RAM (GB)	CPU	Hours	Proc. Data (GiB)	Nodes	Execution Time	Invocations
Compute (CE)	X	X	X	X				
Load Balancer				X	X			
Kubernetes Engine (GKE)	X	X	X			X		
Cloud Functions (CF)		X	X		X		X	X

To obtain information about the resources consumed by the microservices and thus to parameterize the calculator, we run a load test of 1000 requests per second to each microservice, running in a virtual machine. Resource usage was measured with Weave Cloud.

Table 2 details the costs. It is clear that Cloud Functions are the least expensive option.

Table 2. Costs

Service	Type of Machine	RAM (GB)	CPUs	Rules	Processed Data (GiB)	Nodes	Hours × Month	Invocations	Total USD
LB				6	14.2				25.66
GKE	N1	3.75	1			4			97.09
CE	N1	3.75	1				730		24.27
CF	512 MB 800 MHz CPU (CPU)				14.2			35400	5.48

4.2 Implemented Architectures

Google Compute Engine. In the cloud virtual machine environment (IaaS) we have full control over the infrastructure, but it is necessary to install everything needed to run the application. The customer is also responsible for upgrades and secure access services. The virtual machine of our environment was created with Ubuntu 20.04 LTS OS, Java

8 was installed, and we enabled http traffic, which is disabled by default. Additionally, the IP address of the machine was configured to make requests outside Google Cloud. The deployment diagram is shown in Fig. 4.

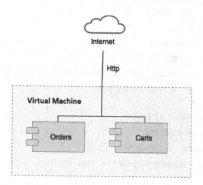

Fig. 4. Components managed in the CE Virtual Machine

Google Kubernetes Engine. The deployment in Kubernetes requires knowledge of their different components and how to describe them in a yaml file. We must write a yaml file for each microservice, where the pods associated to the service and the database are described. Additionally, the port and the Docker image to be used are defined (we use Docker version 0.4.7). Below are the yaml file components. For the service, we need to specify that the type is "Service", in addition to specifying a selector of type "LoadBalancer". Once the yaml file is defined for each microservice, a cluster with the pods and services is created in GKE. In the Fig. 5, the deployment is observed.

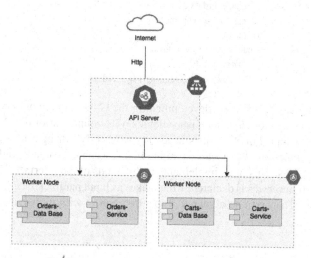

Fig. 5. Google Kubernetes Engine Components

```
apiVersion: v1 kind: Pod
metadata:
    name: orders labels:
        name: orders app:
        orders-app
spec:
        containers:
        - name: orders
          image: weaveworksdemos/orders:0.4.7 ports:
            - container Port:80

apiVersion: v1 kind:
Service metadata:
    name: orders-service labels:
        name: orders-service app: orders-
        app
spec:
    ports:
    - port:80 targetPort: 80
    selector: name:
        orders
        app: orders-app type:

LoadBalancer

apiVersion: v1 kind: Pod
metadata:
    name: orders-db labels:
        name: orders-db
        app: orders-app spec:
    containers:
    - name: orders-db image:
        mongo porst:
        - name: mongo containerPort: 27017
```

Cloud Functions. For the code development in the Cloud Functions service we used the IDE provided by Google, which is available on its online platform.

To create a Cloud Function, it is necessary to specify a trigger-http which is the activator of the function. As we can see in the Fig. 6, a change is made to the microservice controller class. This class implements the methods of the interface *HttpFunction*, where the function *service* is declared, which takes as input parameter a *httpRequest* and a *httpResponse*. The first one allows to know the request with its parameters, and the second one has the response of the request. According to the command *http* received, the corresponding action is performed. To obtain a response from the service, the "set-StatusCode" function is used. Additionally, a *BufferedWriter* object is defined, which allows to have the code as a response as well as the endpoint generated from the deployment. Finally, the following changes were made in the pom.xml configuration file: the Java version was modified from 8 to 11, since the Cloud Functions are available from that version. Subsequently, the Google Cloud Functions dependency was added, and by means of Maven, the corresponding plugin was imported, defining the name of the functions created.

5   Experiments

To evaluate the performance of each microservice in the three selected components of Google Cloud Platform, we generate load using Jmeter. The load consisted in 200, 1000, 1500, 5000 and 10000 requests per second to microservices. Two types of tests were performed: in the first one (Test 1), the mentioned number of requests is sent to each of the microservices. In the second test (Test 2) the number of requests is evenly distributed between the two types of microservices. The performance metric was the response time calculated in milliseconds. The percentage of requests correctly resolved over the total time was also measured.

5.1   Results

In Figs. 7 and 8 we can observe the average response time of the two microservices in the three different architectures, for Tests 1 and 2. It can be observed that as the number of requirements increases the average response time on the virtual machine has a steeper increase until it reaches a maximum of approximately 150000 ms, while on Kubernetes it reaches 50000 ms. The maximum time for Cloud Functions of 30000, showing the most conservative increase as the load increases.

Another variable considered was the number of requests rightly resolved over the total time. As shown in Figs. 9 and 10, in both GKE and CF it is observed that this ratio is always larger than in virtual machines as load increases. This indicates again shorter execution times and a higher number of requirements correctly attended.

```
public class CartsController implements HttpFunction {
private CartDAO cartDAO;

@Override
public void service(HttpRequest request, HttpResponse response)
getQueryParameters()
    throws IOException {
    String params[] = request.getQueryParameters();
    String url = "/carts/" params[0]
    String customerId = params[0]
    if (request.getPath() == url){
        if (request.getMethod() == "GET") {
            BufferedWriter writer = response.getWriter();
            writer.write(CartResource(cartDAO, customerId).value().get());
        }
        if (request.getMethod() == "POST") {
            BufferedWriter writer = response.getWriter();
            writer.write(CartResource(cartDAO, customerId).destroy().run());
        }
    }
    if (request.getPath() == url "/merge"){
        if (request.getMethod() == "GET") {
            String sessionId = params[1]
            logger.debug("Merge carts request received for ids: " + customerId + " and " + sessionId);
            CartResource sessionCart = new CartResource(cartDAO, sessionId);
            CartResource customerCart = new CartResource(cartDAO, customerId);
            customerCart.merge(sessionCart.value().get()).run();
            delete(sessionId);
            BufferedWriter writer = response.getWriter();

        }
    }
}
}
```

Fig. 6. Controller for shopping cart microservice developed with Cloud Functions

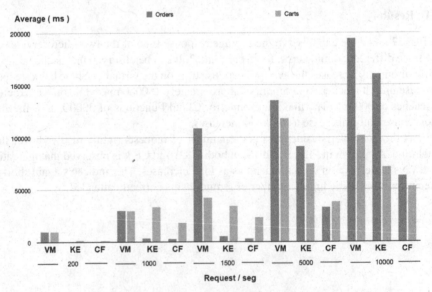

Fig. 7. Test 1 - Average response times

6 Conclusions

In this article we have evaluated three options of a public cloud provider for microservices deployment. The deployment was performed on Google Cloud Platform and two microservices from the Socks Shop benchmark were used. The options evaluated were the Compute Engine, containers orchestrated by Google Kubernetes Engine and Cloud Functions. Virtual machines are a convenient option for those who are unfamiliar with the other technologies mentioned, since all the software needed to run a microservice is installed in the same way as it is done on an on-premise server. The virtual machine is not the best option from a performance and reliability point of view, as observed in the experimental results. Finally, CE is not the cheapest option because you pay for the time the machine is on, whether it is running the microservice or not.

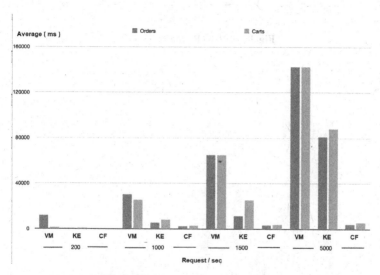

Fig. 8. Test 2 - Average response time

Deployment in GKE is expensive and its performance and reliability results are better than those of CE. It is a suitable service when you know the system and their concepts because you probably already have the microservices running with Kubernetes in an on-premises infrastructure and want to migrate fully to the cloud or use a hybrid scheme. In this case, the migration will offer less effort for programmers and very little change to the application.

Cloud Functions proved to be the least expensive option with better performance indicators as the load increased. It was necessary, however, to understand the philosophy of the functions to introduce small changes to the code. It is important to continue to test these options with all the microservices in the benchmark, as well as with other microservice-based systems. The goal is to test auto-scaling functions (in the event of a load increase) and maintenance of the number of replicas in the event of a microservice failure.

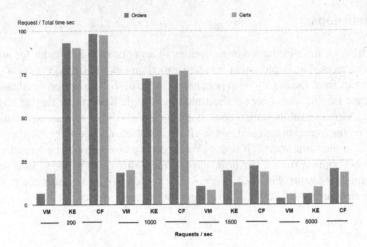

Fig. 9. Test 1 - Requests/total time

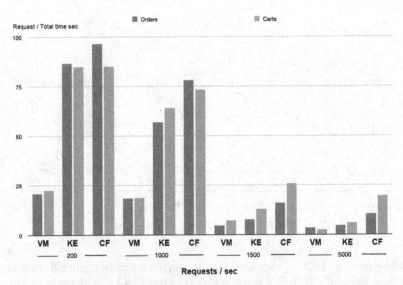

Fig. 10. Test 2 - Requests/total time

References

1. Aderaldo, C.M., Mendonça, N.C., Pahl, C., Jamshidi, P.: Benchmark requirements for microservices architecture research. In: 2017 IEEE/ACM 1st International Workshop on Establishing the Community-Wide Infrastructure for Architecture-Based Software Engineering (ECASE), pp. 8–13. IEEE (2017)
2. Thönes, J.: Microservices. IEEE Softw. **32**(1), 116 (2015)
3. Fowler, M., Lewis, J.: Microservices: Nur ein weiteres konzept in der softwarearchitektur oder mehr. Objektspektrum **1**(2015), 14–20 (2015)
4. Docker. https://www.docker.com/. Accessed 20 Apr 2022

5. Krochmalski, J.: Developing with Docker. Packt Publishing Ltd (2016)
6. Kubernetes. https://kubernetes.io/. Accessed 20 Apr 2022
7. Burns, B., Beda, J., Hightower, K.: Kubernetes. Dpunkt Heidelberg, Germany (2018)
8. Baier, J.: Getting Started with Kubernetes. Community Experience Distilled. Packt Publishing (2017)
9. Qué es la informática sin servidor. https://www.redhat.com/es/topics/cloud-native-apps/what-is-serverless. Accessed 20 Apr 2022
10. Villamizar, M., et al.: Infrastructure cost comparison of running web applications in the cloud using aws lambda and monolithic and microservice architectures. In: 2016 16th IEEE/ACM International Symposium on Cluster, Cloud and Grid Computing (CCGrid), pp. 179–182. IEEE (2016)
11. Fan, C.F., Jindal, A., Gerndt, M.: Microservices vs serverless: a performance comparison on a cloud-native web application. In: CLOSER, pp. 204–215 (2020)
12. Amaral, M., Polo, J., Carrera, D., Mohomed, I., Unuvar, M., Steinder, M.: Performance evaluation of microservices architectures using containers. In: 2015 IEEE 14th International Symposium on Network Computing and Applications, pp. 27–34 (2015). https://doi.org/10.1109/NCA.2015.49
13. Sock shop - microservices-demo. https://microservices-demo.github.io/. Accessed 20 Apr 2022

Epymodel: A User-Friendly Web Application for Visualising COVID-19 Projections for Paraguay Including Under-Reporting and Vaccination

José Luis Vázquez Noguera[1]([✉])[iD], Hyun Ho Shin[2,3][iD], Carlos Sauer Ayala[4][iD], Sebastián Grillo[5][iD], Pastor Pérez-Estigarribia[6][iD], Ricardo Torales[5][iD], Silvia Vázquez Noguera[7][iD], and Carlos Gaona[2][iD]

[1] Ingeniería Informática, Universidad Americana, 1206 Asunción, Paraguay
jose.vazquez@ua.edu.py
[2] Núcleo de Investigación y Desarrollo Tecnológico, Universidad Nacional de Asunción, 111421 San Lorenzo, Paraguay
hshin@pol.una.py, hshin@qui.una.py,
carlos.federico005@fpuna.edu.py
[3] Departamento de Aplicaciones Industriales, Facultad de Ciencias Químicas, Universidad Nacional de Asunción, 111421 San Lorenzo, Paraguay
[4] Departamento de Ingeniería Industrial, Universidad Nacional de Asunción, 111421 San Lorenzo, Paraguay
csauer@ing.una.py
[5] Facultad de Ciencias y Tecnologías, Universidad Autónoma de Asunción, 1013 Asunción, Paraguay
{sgrillo,rtorales}@uaa.edu.py
[6] Facultad de Medicina, Universidad Sudamericana, Asunción, Paraguay
pastor.perez@sudamericana.edu.py
[7] Facultad de Ciencias Económicas y Administrativas, Universidad Nacional de Concepción, Concepción, Paraguay
svazquez@fcea-unc.edu.py

Abstract. Most health software fails due to the lack of efficient use. Moreover, the appearance of COVID-19 has generated the need for a user-friendly system that allows us to visualise possible scenarios of contagion, hospitalised patients and deaths. Previous work addressed the mathematical modelling of the spread dynamics and its impact in the public health system with time-dependent transmissibility and proportions using a moving time-window strategy. In this work, we extend the mathematical model to include an estimate of under-reported COVID-19 cases and the immunisation impact from vaccination campaigns. The model parameters are estimated using a Bayesian approach with data from Paraguay and are compared to those obtained in a previous work. The comparisons show that the proposed model can better explain the different circumstances observed from Paraguay since June 2021, when the under-reporting and vaccinations effects become essential. Some scenarios are drawn based on the historical transmissibility and are assessed using the observed data. A web application called Epymodel was developed to show both the historical values of the parameters and variables

V. Agredo-Delgado et al. (Eds.): CCC 2022, CCIS 1775, pp. 58–72, 2023.
https://doi.org/10.1007/978-3-031-36357-3_5

of the proposed model, as well as the projections of the different scenarios. Finally, a usability test of the web application is performed. Users showed a high level of satisfaction in the use of Epymodel.

Keywords: mathematical modelling · COVID-19 · under-reporting · vaccination · web application · usability

1 Introduction

The COVID-19 pandemic shows that understanding the behaviour of the epidemic is of interest not only to epidemiological modelling specialists, but also to physicians, decision-makers and a public whose mathematical knowledge base is limited. In this sense, the appropriate communication of forecasts obtained from mathematical models constitutes a challenge itself, in addition to the epidemiological phenomenon modelling [1].

Web applications constitute a way of communicating epidemiological information. On these, their forecasts can vary based on assumptions, such as optimistic, pessimistic or moderate, that the user must understand [2, 3]. This is, web platforms for epidemiological models go beyond simple static graphics and require varying degrees of user interaction, so that the user can obtain the required information in a simple, clear, and fast way. In a more general sense, we encounter challenges similar to the use of any web platform, *i.e.*, the problem of web usability [4].

The COVID-19 pandemic also motivated the development of epidemiological models based on the traditional SIR/SEIR (SIR: Susceptible-Infectious-Recovered/SEIR: Susceptible-Exposed-Infectious-Recovered) models. These proposals considered aspects such as the number of deaths, quarantined, hospital dynamics, under-reporting and vaccination [5–9]. In order to better understand the long-term behaviour of COVID-19 in a population, the degree of immunity to the virus is particularly important: The estimation of under-reporting cases of COVID-19 can add the natural immunity in the population [10]; at the same time, artificial immunity obtained from vaccines became essential in most countries [11]. Thus, from the SEIR-H model, previously published in [12], which modelled the spread of COVID-19 and the hospital dynamics with time-varying transmissibility and proportions, here, we propose the estimation of under-reporting and vaccination effects into the dynamic model. This extended model is called SEIR-HV. As in [12], the model proposed in this work and the developed web application aim to help policymakers to design better policies in the management of the present pandemic as well as for future epidemics.

The parameters of the proposed model are estimated using a Bayesian approach with moving time-window strategy [12]. We perform an analysis of the SEIR-HV model, comparing it with the SEIR-H model with respect to transmissibility, the percentage of susceptible, and the proportion of infected who are hospitalised. The comparative analysis between models shows large differences from one model values to another. Several projection scenarios are drawn based on the historical transmissibility, which are simulated with the SEIR-HV model and assessed using the observed data.

A web application called Epymodel (http://epymodel.uaa.edu.py/) was developed to show the historical values of the parameters, as well as the projections of the different scenarios. A usability test is performed to the Epymodel web application, and the efficacy and satisfaction results obtained are presented.

This article is organised as follows: in Sect. 2, a brief description of SEIR-HV model with parameter estimation methodology are presented; also, the Epymodel web application with the scenarios and the methodology of usability testing are presented. In Sect. 3, the estimated parameters, the comparisons between models, and the assessment of different scenarios are given and discussed; then, the results of usability testing are also presented and discussed. Finally, some final remarks are given in Conclusion.

2 Materials and Methods

In this section, we describe the SEIR-HV model and the methodology for parameter estimation. Since the SEIR-HV model is based on the SEIR-H model we emphasise new features and refer to [12] for details. The description of the Epymodel web application with the projection scenarios and the usability testing methodology are given.

2.1 Mathematical Model

The SEIR-H model assumes a time-dependent transmissibility considering the combined effects of the variability in the social behaviour and COVID-19 variants [12]. The SEIR-HV model incorporates the estimates of under-reported cases and the effect of vaccination campaigns in SEIR-H model. Thus, the SEIR-HV model is expressed as (see Fig. 1):

$$\frac{dS}{dt} = -\beta \frac{S}{N} I - \eta V_{\text{filtered}} + \psi O, \tag{1}$$

$$\frac{dE}{dt} = \beta \frac{S}{N} I - \alpha E, \tag{2}$$

$$\frac{dI}{dt} = \alpha E - \gamma I, \tag{3}$$

$$\frac{dC}{dt} = \gamma I + R_{im}, \tag{4}$$

$$\frac{dH}{dt} = \lambda_{IH} \gamma I - \lambda_{HU} \delta_{HU} H - \lambda_{HF} \delta_{HF} H - \lambda_{HO} \delta_{HO} H, \tag{5}$$

$$\frac{dU}{dt} = \lambda_{HU} \delta_{HU} H - \lambda_{UF} \varphi_{UF} U - \lambda_{UO} \varphi_{UO} U, \tag{6}$$

$$\frac{dF}{dt} = \lambda_{IF} \gamma I + \lambda_{HF} \delta_{HF} H + \lambda_{UF} \varphi_{UF} U, \tag{7}$$

$$\frac{dO}{dt} = \lambda_{IO} \gamma I + \lambda_{HO} \delta_{HO} H + \lambda_{UO} \varphi_{UO} U + \eta V_{\text{filtered}} - \psi O, \tag{8}$$

where S is the susceptible group, E exposed (latent stage), I are infectious, C are the cumulative cases which includes the reported R and the estimation of under-reported,

R_{im} are the cases reported in the group of travellers from abroad, H are the hospitalised, U those are admitted in Intensive Care Unit (ICU), F are the cumulative deaths, and O are those who are recovered and possess immunity. The initial population N is maintained constant in time.

The daily reported cases $\Delta R = R - R(t - 1)$ are scaled by a varying under-reporting factor f as follows: $\Delta C = f\Delta R$, where $\Delta C = C - C(t - 1)$ refers to the estimated daily new cases including those under-reported. This under-reporting factor f is estimated outside SEIR-HV. The detailed description is presented in Sect. 2.2.

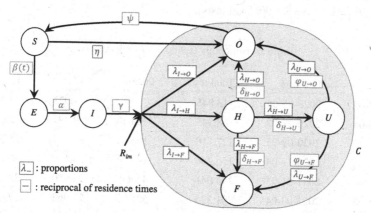

Fig. 1. Schematic diagrams of the proposed model: The green region corresponds to the cumulative cases.

The under-reporting factor is estimated outside SEIR-HV. For this purpose, the epidemic period in Paraguay is divided at bimonthly intervals, where in each interval a value of under-reporting factor is estimated using the semi-Bayesian probabilistic bias analysis proposed by Wu et al. [13].

The value $V_{filtered}$ stands for the exponential smoothing [14] of the vaccination data (full dose) [15], with the smoothing constant 1/14 for the immune response [16]. The parameter $\eta = 0.9$ is the overall effectiveness of the vaccine, and $\psi = 1/360$ is the reciprocal of the immunity loss assuming an annual emergence of new COVID-19 Variants of Concern (VOC) [17].

The parameters to be estimated are the transmissibility β, and the proportions λ_* (with $* \in \{IH, IF, HU, HF, UF\}$) for the dynamics of bed occupations in hospitals. The parameter λ_{AB} indicates the proportion of the compartment A that is transferred into B, and $\sum_{i,i\backslash neqA}\lambda_{Ai} = 1$. . (See Table 1 of [12] for other parameters). The detailed description of parameter estimation is given in Sect. 2.3.

2.2 Under-Reporting Factor

In this subsection, the methodology of estimation of under-reporting factor and the results are presented. Here, the semi-Bayesian probabilistic bias analysis proposed by Wu et al. [13] is used to estimate the under-reporting factor at different times of the epidemic in

Paraguay at bimonthly intervals. Then, using a statistical hypothesis testing approach, we infer an empirical model that allows us to estimate the under-reporting factor as a function of the testing rate per day and/or positivity.

The implementation in R [18] by Wu et al. [13] is adapted to estimate the under-reporting factor at bimonthly intervals using the data from Paraguay. Table 1 shows the data and intervals used for the estimations, where, the test rate T* is defined as the total number of tests performed in a time interval (two months) per a thousand population in the same area (T* = Total tests ×1000/N) and, the positive rate P* is defined as the percentage of reported cases over the total number of tests performed in the same time interval (P* = Positive × 100/Total tests).

Table 1. Bimonthly testing effort in Paraguay

Start date	End date	Total tests	Positive	T*	P*
2020-03-09	2020-05-08	13,845	562	1.923	4.1%
2020-05-08	2020-07-07	68,345	2,040	9.492	3.0%
2020-07-07	2020-09-05	127,118	19,415	17.655	15.3%
2020-09-05	2020-11-04	170,266	44,604	23.648	26.2%
2020-11-04	2021-01-03	194,041	44,445	26.950	22.9%
2021-01-03	2021-03-04	201,324	55,592	27.962	27.6%
2021-03-04	2021-05-03	352,711	121,745	48.988	34.5%
2021-05-03	2021-07-02	434,447	143,780	60.340	33.1%

For each bimonthly data of the Table 1, a factor f (defined as a ratio between the estimated infections and the confirmed reported cases) is determined using the methodology presented in [13]. The prior distributions for the probabilistic bias analysis are used without modification. Thus, based on previous these bimonthly under-reported cases estimates, the statistical models for the factor f as a function of an average number of tests per day $\overline{T}$ and/or an average number of positive rate per day $\overline{P}$. Given the observed trend pattern, the following models were contrasted: $f = a\overline{T}^{b}$; $f = ae^{b\overline{T}}$; $f = a\overline{P}^{b}$; $f = ae^{b\overline{P}}$; $f = a\overline{T}^{b}\overline{P}^{c}$; $f = a\overline{T}^{b}e^{c\overline{P}}$; $f = ae^{b\overline{T}}e^{c\overline{P}}$, where a, b and c are unknown parameters estimated using log-linear and linear regression. To find which of these models best explains f, we use performance metrics that penalise the number of unknown parameters by minimising the bias and the number of variables in the model. These metrics were estimated using the `compareLM` [19] and `compare_performance` [20] functions implemented in R [18].

2.3 Parameter Estimation

For parameter estimation, we adopt the methodology from [12]. Besides the daily records of reported cases from travellers $R_{im}(t)$, hospital bed occupation $D^{H}(t)$, ICU occupation $D^{U}(t)$, and the cumulative reported $D^{R}(t)$ and deaths $D^{F}(t)$, which are used in [12], we include the daily tests performed T(t) from the Health Monitoring Centre in Paraguay (http://dgvs.mspbs.gov.py/, accessed on 22 December 2021) and the vaccination data V(t) from [15]. The daily records of reported cases are denoted as $D^{\Delta R}(t)$ and the daily deaths as $D^{\Delta F}(t)$. The estimates of daily new cases $D^{\Delta C}$ are obtained using the under-reporting factor $f(t)$ by applying $D^{\Delta C}(t_j) = f(t_j)D^{\Delta R}(t_j)$, for each day t_j.

Strong containment policies adopted by the government, between the first confirmed COVID-19 case in Paraguay $t_0 = 7$ March 2020 and $t_{nn} = 5$ October 2020, resulted in low hospital bed occupations. For this time interval, compartments associated with the hospitalisations are not considered, remaining Eqs. (1)–(4) with a modification of Eq. (8) into:

$$\frac{dO(t)}{dt} = \gamma I(t) + \eta V_{filtered}(t) - \psi O(t). \tag{9}$$

Since $t_{nn} = 5$ October 2020, when the measures are relaxed, the fully coupled set of Eqs. (1)–(8) are used to estimate parameters, requiring adjustments to the methodology described in [12]. The estimation of the parameter set $\{\beta_j, \lambda_{*j}\}$ at time $t_j \geq t_{nn}$ is performed using the Bayesian method:

$$P\left(\beta_j, \lambda_{*j}, \sigma_j^+ | D_j^X\right) \propto P\left(D_j^X | \beta_j, \lambda_{*j}, \sigma_j^+\right) P\left(\beta_j, \lambda_{*j}, \sigma_j^+\right). \tag{10}$$

It is assumed that the data $D_j^X = \{D_j^{\Delta C}, D_j^H, D_j^U, D_j^{\Delta F}\}$ are independent, thus the likelihood in the Eq. (10) is a product of four likelihoods: $P\left(D_j^{X_i} | \beta_j, \lambda_{*j}, \sigma_j^{+i}\right)$ for $X_i = \{\Delta C, H, U, \Delta F\}$ and $+_i = \{C, H, U, F\}$, respectively. For more precise values of transmissibility, the likelihood corresponding to the transmissibility is augmented by a factor of three. For the likelihoods, we assume that the data are normal-distributed around the simulation results with the mentioned parameter set.

2.4   Website with Projections

A user-friendly web application called Epymodel (http://epymodel.uaa.edu.py/) was developed for visualisation of COVID-19 projections. Table 2 shows the tools employed for the development of the web application.

Table 2. Tools used to develop the web application.

Tool	Use
Python 3.7.4	Programming language of the back-end
Django 2.2.10	Back-end Framework
Bootstrap 3.0	Front-end framework (for responsive page design)
D3 3.0	Front-end framework (for graphics presentation)

Epymodel shows projections for Paraguay of (i) daily reported cases; (ii) hospital bed occupation; (iii) ICU occupation; (iv) daily deceased; also the estimated transmissibility and proportions from the SEIR-HV model with their credible intervals.

For the projections, two groups of scenarios with three scenarios in each group are presented:

1. Scenarios with historical transmissibility in Paraguay:
- **Plateau**: The transmissibility that gives the effective reproduction number equal to one is considered.
- **Percentile 25** uses the percentile 25 of last year (if possible) historic transmissibility.
- **Percentile 75** uses the percentile 75 of last year historic transmissibility.
2. Scenarios associated with current measures.
- **Last month's measures** considers the average transmissibility of the last month; it assumes the continuity of the current measures.
- **10% increase/relaxation** increases by 10% from the average transmissibility of the last two weeks; it corresponds to the slight relaxation of the measures.
- **20% reduction/containment** decreases by 20% from the average transmissibility of the last two weeks; it considers the containment of the measures.

The Sigmoid function with a variation width $W/2 = 7$ days is used in order to join the latest estimated transmissibility to the transmissibility considered in each scenario; the proportions λ_* and the under-reporting factor $f(t)$ are maintained constant with the latest estimated values. Only, in the pessimistic scenarios, "Percentile 75" and "10% increase" the proportions λ_* are augmented by 10% when the effective Reproduction number is larger than one.

2.5 Epymodel: Usability Testing

The usability of the Epymodel web application was tested based on two fundamental principles: efficacy, to measure by means of binary success whether a user is able to perform tasks [21], and satisfaction, to measure the positive attitude in the use of the web application by means of a System Usability Scale (SUS) [22].

3 Results and Discussion

The results obtained based on the methodology described above are presented. The estimated parameters are shown and compared to those obtained with SEIR-H model [12]; and the assessment of the scenarios is presented. Finally, the results of usability are shown.

3.1 Determination of Under-Reporting Factor

Figure 2 shows the results of the factor of estimated infections vs. confirmed cases from the Probabilistic bias analysis. Overall, there is an inverse relationship between the test rate per day and the under-reporting factor. Similarly, positivity and under-reporting factor are inversely proportional. However, these trends are not linear.

Table 3 shows the results of model comparison for the under-reporting factor as a function of average testing rate per day and/or the positive rate. The models are log-linearised. AICc is the corrected Akaike Information Criterion, expressed as:

$$\text{AICc} = 2k + n \ln L + \frac{2k^2 + 2k}{n-k-1}, \tag{11}$$

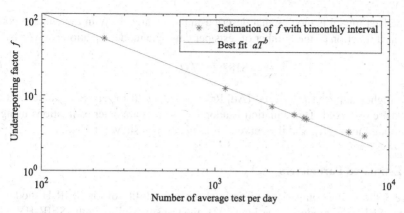

Fig. 2. A log–log relationship of under-reporting factor and tests per day.

where L is the maximum likelihood function, k is the number of unknown (free) parameters of the model and n is the number of data. The AICc values allow comparison between models, using the expression:

$$w_{i,j} = e^{(\text{AICc}_i - \text{AICc}_j)/2}, \tag{12}$$

which is interpreted as the probability that the j-th model fitted to the data minimises the loss of information compared to the i-th model with lower AICc. R-squared (R^2) is a measure of the proportion of the variance of a dependent variable that is explained by an independent variable or variables in a regression model. Adjusted R-squared (Adj.R^2) is a modified version of R-squared that has been adjusted for the number of predictors in the model.

Table 3. Best model performance for factor of estimated infection vs. confirmed cases

f model	Df.res	AICc	Adj.R^2
$\log(f) = \log(a) + b\log(\overline{T})$	6	−7.63	0.99
$\log(f) = \log(a) + b\log(\overline{T}) + c\overline{P}$	5	−0.91	0.99
$\log(f) = \log(a) + b\log(\overline{T}) + c\log(\overline{P})$	5	1.40	0.99
$\log(f) = \log(a) + b\overline{P}$	6	21.57	0.71
$\log(f) = \log(a) + b\log(\overline{P})$	6	22.39	0.68
$\log(f) = \log(a) + b\overline{T}$	6	23.22	0.64
$\log(f) = \log(a) + b\overline{T} + c\overline{P}$	5	30.33	0.68

The best model is the one that describes a power-law decay in the under-reporting factor as a function of the number of tests per day. The model equation is given by:

$$f(t) = 8183.785\,T(t)^{-0.914773},\tag{13}$$

where higher adjusted R-squared (Adj.$R^2 = 0.99$) with lower AICc value (AICc $= -7.63$) are observed. This equation is adopted for the parameter estimations using the data of daily tests $T(t)$, and the curve of this equation is shown in Fig. 2.

3.2 Estimated Parameters

Figure 3 shows the comparison of optimal transmissibility of the SEIR-H model [12] with the SEIR-HV model. Since June 2021, the transmissibility in the SEIR-HV model diverges from the SEIR-H model. This is mainly due to the differences in the susceptible populations for both models (see Fig. 4 (left)): by June, in the SEIR-HV model, it drops to 85%, and continues to decrease mainly due to the larger vaccinations available around June 2021, but in the SEIR-H model, it is almost constant from June 2021.

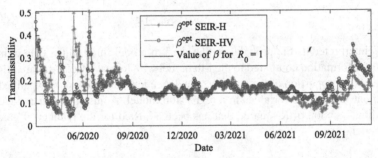

Fig. 3. Optimal transmissibility: Comparison between SEIR-HV and SEIR-H model.

The transmissibility shown in Fig. 3 confirms the adequacy of the SEIR-H model until May 2021, when the susceptible population is still large. But, when a considerable number of the population has acquired immunity, it is necessary to include the effects of immunisation in the modelling for more realistic simulations.

In May 2021 and for more than a month, reported daily deaths reached on average 13 deaths per million, some days peaking at 21 deaths per million. This could have influenced the population to be more cautious in hygiene and distancing practices, effectively reducing transmissibility in July and August 2021. However, as more people received the second dose of the vaccine, mobility returned almost to pre-pandemic levels, and transmissibility increased starting in late August 2021. But still, daily cases and deaths remained low for at least two months (0.6 deaths per million). This can be attributed to the reduction of susceptible population, and people still maintaining distancing and hygiene practices.

Figure 4 (right) shows the optimal proportion from the infectious I to the hospitalised H (λ_{IH}) for both models. Only this proportion is shown, because there are no appreciable

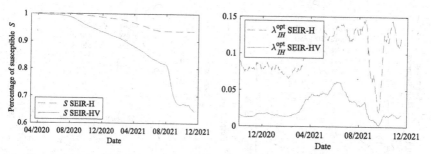

Fig. 4. Comparison between SEIR-HV and SEIR-H model: Percentage of susceptible S (left), and optimal proportion from I to H, λ_{IH} (right).

differences in other proportions between both models. Lower values can be observed for the SEIR-HV model since under-reporting is now considered. In fact, some studies show that the hospitalisation proportions of infected are about 2% [23], which is better represented by the SEIR-HV model. Also, SEIR-HV shows smaller oscillations which are more realistic.

3.3 Assessment of the Scenarios

The pessimistic scenarios "Percentile 75" and "10% increase" define upper limits, and the optimistic scenarios "Percentile 25" and "20% reduction" define lower limits. The assessment of the scenarios is performed by measuring the degree of how far the observed data are outside these limits.

The data located above the pessimistic scenarios are measured by:

$$rel\_error_{X,j}^{scn_p}(t_k) = max\left\{\frac{D_j^X(t_k) - Z_j^{X,scn_p}(t_k)}{Z_j^{X,scn_p}(t_k)}, 0\right\}, \tag{14}$$

where X stands for daily reported, hospitalised, ICU or daily deaths, D are data and Z are simulation results for a pessimistic scenario, $scn_p = \{$"Percentile 75", "10% increase"$\}$, using the parameters estimated at day t_j (considering data from t_{j+1} to t_{j+w}), and $t_k = t_{j+w+k} - t_{j+w} = 1, 2, \ldots, 45$ are the projection days. The data of daily reported and daily deaths are filtered using a 7-days moving average. This relative error shows how much the pessimistic scenarios underestimated the observed data. Similarly, to show how the optimistic scenarios overestimated the observed data we define:

$$rel\_error_{X,j}^{scn_o}(t_k) = min\left\{\frac{D_j^X(t_k) - Z_j^{X,scn_o}(t_k)}{Z_j^{X,scn_o}(t_k)}, 0\right\}, \tag{15}$$

where the simulation results are obtained considering the optimistic scenario, $scn_o = \{$"Percentile 25", "20% decrease"$\}$.

Figure 5 show the assessment of the scenarios by averaging the relative error shown in the Eqs. (14)–(15):

$$\overline{rel\_error}_X^{scn_{\{o,p\}}}(t_k) = \frac{1}{N_j}\sum_j rel\_error_{X,j}^{scn_{\{o,p\}}}(t_k), \tag{16}$$

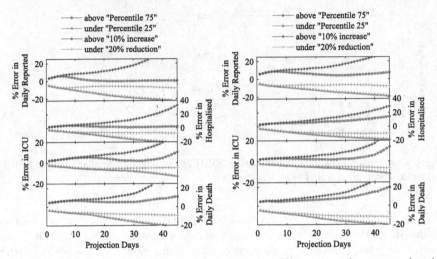

Fig. 5. Error in percentage of the simulation results using different scenarios compared to the observed data, using the SEIR-H model proposed in [12] (left), and using SEIR-HV model proposed in this work (right)

where 7 October 2020 $\leq$ j $\leq$ 8 September 2021, and N_j is the number of days, using both models, the one proposed by Shin et al. [12] and the one proposed in this work, respectively. The projection days are extended to 45 days, but it can be observed that the projections are mostly unreliable above 35–40 days for both models. This is inevitable because the scenarios are drawn considering almost constant parameters.

The scenarios associated with historical transmissibility (percentile 25/percentile 75) are better assessed by the SEIR-H model, while the scenarios based on current measures (10% increase/20% reduction) are better estimated by the SEIR-HV model. It is worth to mention that the modifications included to obtain the SEIR-HV model are related to long-term behaviour. However, scenarios drawn in this work as well as the ones in [12], consider constant transmissibility which is more adequate for short-term behaviour of this pandemic, where changes in social contacts and hygiene recommendations are observed in shorter time. On average, the error is less than 20% in 30 days of projections.

3.4 Usability

Six users (see Table 4 for the profiles) volunteered and performed 21 tasks concerned to Epymodel. This number of users for usability testing is enough because a test with only five participants can show almost 85% of the problems [24]. The tasks consisted of performing consultations on the number of reported, hospitalised or deceased in specific date ranges, hiding or displaying curves in certain graphs, or identifying the tendency that certain curves may have.

Efficacy Measurement. The results show high task accomplishment by users using Epymodel. Figure 6 shows a bar chart, where the vertical axis indicates the number of users, and the horizontal axis the tasks assigned per user. Users were able to obtain

Table 4. Profile of evaluators

Age	Level of study	Labor area	Age	Level of study	Labor area
35	Bachelor's Degree	Nursing	45	Master's Degree	University professor
38	Doctor	Biological Sciences	49	Master's Degree	University professor
33	Master's Degree	University professor	49	Master's Degree	Economic Sciences

and visualise data simulated by the model in specific date ranges. At the same time, users were able to hide curves that they did not need to visualise. Only one task was not achieved by most users (Task 12). This task consists of obtaining the projected number of deaths for the scenario "20% reduction" and "Percentile 75" in 15 July 2021. Users did not realise that to obtain data for a specific date, the mouse could be positioned on that date.

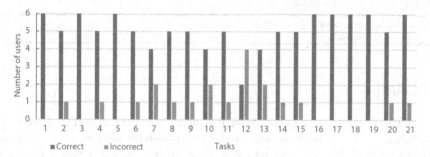

Fig. 6. Results obtained from the Efficacy tests

Satisfaction Measurement. The SUS questionnaire results reveal a high user satisfaction in using Epymodel (see Table 5). The cell values indicate the number of users who have every level of satisfaction for each question. Odd numbered questions evaluate positive aspects in the use of the application, and even questions the opposite. Therefore, a higher level of satisfaction is expected for odd questions, with the opposite being true for even questions.

Users found Epymodel to have a high level of consistency. In turn, they are confident that most people would learn to use the web application very quickly. It is worth noting that users reported that they felt very safe using the system. According to the results obtained, we can conclude that the Epymodel is a user-friendly web application.

Table 5. Results of the SUS questionnaire

Question	Strongly disagree	Disagree	Neutral	Agree	Strongly agree
1. I think that I would like to use this system frequently.	0	0	0	3	3
2. I found the system unnecessarily complex.	2	2	1	0	1
3. I thought the system was easy to use.	0	0	0	4	2
4. I think that I would need the support of a technical person to be able to use this system.	2	2	2	0	0
5. I found the various functions in this system were well integrated.	0	0	0	4	2
6. I thought there was too much inconsistency in this system.	5	0	1	0	0
7. I would imagine that most people would learn to use this system very quickly.	0	0	1	5	0
8. I found the system very cumbersome to use.	3	1	2	0	0
9. I felt very confident using the system.	0	0	0	5	1
10. I needed to learn a lot of things before I could get going with this system.	2	2	1	0	1

4 Conclusions

The SEIR-HV model is proposed. Since this model is an extension of SEIR-H model (published in [12]), strengths as time-varying transmissibility and proportions of spread through hospital dynamics are inherited. Furthermore, for better representation of dynamics, the under-reporting estimation and vaccination effects are incorporated in the proposed model.

The parameters of the proposed model are estimated using the data of Paraguay. These estimated parameters are compared with those obtained from the SEIR-H model. The comparisons show that the proposed model can better explain the different circumstances observed in Paraguay. This is, the inclusion of the under-reporting estimation and vaccination effects seems to become essential from June 2021 where transmissibilities change substantially compared to the previous model.

The assessment of the scenarios shows good results in short-term projections: On average, the pessimistic scenarios underpredict the observed data in less than 20% in 30 days of projections.

Using the SEIR-HV model and scenarios, a user-friendly web application called Epymodel was developed. This application was evaluated in terms of efficacy and satisfaction with several users. The evaluation results indicate that users can achieve their objectives in a satisfactory way.

The developed web application is currently used by the technicians from the Health Monitoring Centre in Paraguay, comparing the results shown by our Epymodel web application with other web applications with similar functionalities.

The scenarios considered in this work are short-term scenarios. It would be necessary to develop and include some mechanisms or functions to vary the transmissibility and proportions considered in the SEIR-HV model for long-term assessment of the pandemic behaviour.

Fundings. This publication has been prepared with the support of CONACYT and UAA, within the grant PINV20-40. The contents of this publication are the sole responsibility of the authors and cannot be taken to reflect the opinion of CONACYT.

References

1. Matta, G.: Science communication as a preventative tool in the COVID19 pandemic. Humanit. Soc. Sci. Commun. **7**, 159 (2020). https://doi.org/10.1057/s41599-020-00645-1
2. Institute for Health Metrics and Evaluation (IHME) IHME: COVID-19 projections. In: Institute for Health Metrics and Evaluation. https://covid19.healthdata.org. Accessed 26 Dec 2021
3. Gu, Y.: COVID-19 projections using machine learning. In: COVID-19 Projections Using Machine Learning. https://covid19-projections.com. Accessed 26 Dec 2021
4. Esmeria, G.J., Seva, R.R.: Web usability: a literature review. In: DLSU Research Congress Proceedings 2017. De La Salle University, Manila, Philippines (2017)
5. López, L., Rodo, X.: A modified SEIR model to predict the COVID-19 outbreak in Spain and Italy: simulating control scenarios and multi-scale epidemics. Results Phys. **21**, 103746 (2021). https://doi.org/10.1016/j.rinp.2020.103746
6. Mwalili, S., Kimathi, M., Ojiambo, V., Gathungu, D., Mbogo, R.: SEIR model for COVID-19 dynamics incorporating the environment and social distancing. BMC Res. Notes **13**, 352 (2020). https://doi.org/10.1186/s13104-020-05192-1
7. Calafiore, G.C., Novara, C., Possieri, C.: A modified SIR model for the COVID-19 contagion in Italy. In: 2020 59th IEEE Conference on Decision and Control (CDC). IEEE, Jeju, Korea (South) (2020)
8. Cooper, I., Mondal, A., Antonopoulos, C.G.: A SIR model assumption for the spread of COVID-19 in different communities. Chaos Solitons Fractals **139**, 110057 (2020). https://doi.org/10.1016/j.chaos.2020.110057
9. Chen, Y.-C., Lu, P.-E., Chang, C.-S., Liu, T.-H.: A Time-Dependent SIR model for COVID-19 with undetectable infected persons. IEEE Trans. Netw. Sci. Eng. **7**, 3279–3294 (2020). https://doi.org/10.1109/TNSE.2020.3024723
10. Lau, H., Khosrawipour, T., Kocbach, P., Ichii, H., Bania, J., Khosrawipour, V.: Evaluating the massive underreporting and undertesting of COVID-19 cases in multiple global epicenters. Pulmonology **27**, 110–115 (2021). https://doi.org/10.1016/j.pulmoe.2020.05.015
11. Yavuz, M., Coşar, F.Ö., Günay, F., Özdemir, F.N.: A new mathematical modeling of the COVID-19 pandemic including the vaccination campaign. Open J. Modell. Simul. **09**, 299–321 (2021). https://doi.org/10.4236/ojmsi.2021.93020
12. Shin, H.H., et al.: A mathematical model for COVID-19 with variable transmissibility and hospitalizations: a case study in Paraguay. Appl. Sci. **11**, 9726 (2021). https://doi.org/10.3390/app11209726
13. Wu, S.L., et al.: Substantial underestimation of SARS-CoV-2 infection in the United States. Nat. Commun. **11**, 1 (2020). https://doi.org/10.1038/s41467-020-18272-4

14. Brown, R.G.: Smoothing, forecasting and prediction of discrete time series. Courier Corporation (2004)
15. Mathieu, E., et al.: A global database of COVID-19 vaccinations. Nat. Hum. Behav. **5**, 947–953 (2021). https://doi.org/10.1038/s41562-021-01122-8
16. Bar-On, Y.M., et al.: Protection of BNT162b2 vaccine booster against COVID-19 in Israel. N. Engl. J. Med. **385**, 1393–1400 (2021). https://doi.org/10.1056/NEJMoa2114255
17. Rubin, R.: COVID-19 vaccines vs variants–determining how much immunity is enough. JAMA **325**, 1241–1243 (2021). https://doi.org/10.1001/jama.2021.3370
18. Core Team, R.R.: R: A Language and Environment for Statistical Computing (2021)
19. Mangiafico, S.: rcompanion: Functions to Support Extension Education Program Evaluation (2021)
20. Lüdecke, D., Ben-Shachar, M.S., Patil, I., Waggoner, P., Makowski, D.: Performance: an R package for assessment, comparison and testing of statistical models. J. Open Source Softw. **6**, 3139 (2021). https://doi.org/10.21105/joss.03139
21. Albert, W., Tullis, T.: Measuring the User Experience: Collecting, Analyzing, and Presenting Usability Metrics, 2nd edn. Elsevier, Amsterdam, Netherlands (2013)
22. Lewis, J.R.: The system usability scale: past, present, and future. Int. J. Hum. Comput. Interact. **34**, 577–590 (2018). https://doi.org/10.1080/10447318.2018.1455307
23. Menachemi, N., Dixon, B.E., Wools-Kaloustian, K.K., Yiannoutsos, C.T., Halverson, P.K.: How many SARS-CoV-2–infected people require hospitalization? Using random sample testing to better inform preparedness efforts. J. Public Health Manag. Pract. **27**, 246–250 (2021). https://doi.org/10.1097/PHH.0000000000001331
24. Nielsen, J.: Why you only need to test with 5 users (2000). https://www.nngroup.com/articles/why-you-only-need-to-test-with-5-users/. Accessed 26 Dec 2021

Expert System for Software Architecture Selection

Leonardo Bermon-Angarita$^{(\boxtimes)}$ (iD), Néstor Darío Duque-Méndez(iD),
and Claudia Patricia Ríos-Ruiz

Departamento de Informática y Computación, Universidad Nacional de Colombia Sede
Manizales, Manizales, Caldas, Colombia
{lbermona,ndduqueme,cpriosr}@unal.edu.co

Abstract. Architectural design is a fundamental stage of the software development process. During this design, the highest level components that make up the software product and their relationships between them are determined. However, many architectures, patterns, and architectural styles are not easy to select according to the non-functional requirements of a software development project. Therefore, innovative approaches are required to support the software architect in making decisions about an appropriate architecture. This work presents an expert system based on a set of rules that supports the selection of a certain software architecture according to the non-functional requirements, which are the input variables of the system. The results show that the expert system developed is an easy tool to learn and use, together with a good quality of the decisions recommended to support the selection of a software architecture of a software project based on its identified non-functional requirements.

Keywords: Software architecture · Architectural style · Expert system

1 Introduction

Software architecture is the components, behaviors, and relationships that influence the abstractions of a software system by providing a mechanism for reasoning about key features such as maintainability, scalability, security, performance, portability, etc. [1]. The use of a good software architecture is fundamental for the design, taking into account the organization and communication of the system's non-functional requirements, which can be influenced by individual components, without neglecting that the architecture is the dominant influence [2].

The evaluation of an architectural design is done by determining how well the system meets the functional and non-functional requirements while it is running [3]. It is common for users to propose a series of non-functional requirements as general goals of the project with limitations on the functions offered by the software system [4].

Knowledge of software architecture is quite broad, specialized, heterogeneous, dispersed, and expressed at different levels of abstraction. Thus, architectural design is limited by the architect's own skills, experience, and a subset of knowledge mastered

V. Agredo-Delgado et al. (Eds.): CCC 2022, CCIS 1775, pp. 73–86, 2023.
https://doi.org/10.1007/978-3-031-36357-3_6

by him. A great effort is required to adjust such knowledge to a specific development scenario [5].

A possible solution to support the task of selecting a suitable software architecture for a given software project is to develop solutions based on artificial intelligence. Within the branches of artificial intelligence, there are expert systems, which reflect the strategies of a human expert in solving problems and have proven their effectiveness in supporting decision-making [6]. For the design of expert systems, it is necessary to capture and codify the knowledge and reasoning of the expert in the form of rules and facts [7].

The selection of a certain software architecture is mainly based on the collection of non-functional requirements defined for the software product to be built. However, the collection of architectural styles and patterns is quite wide and these reference architectures operate at a higher level of abstraction for a set of systems in specific domains [8, 9], which can lead to select architectures inconsistent or inappropriate. Hence the importance of having expert systems that support the software architect in the initial phases of software design.

In this work, the development of a software tool based on artificial intelligence is proposed, aimed at providing a certain autonomy necessary to determine and recommend the appropriate software architecture based on the non-functional requirements of a software development project.

The paper is organized as follows. The second section presents the background. The third section shows the related works. The fourth section describes the process of developing the expert system. The fifth section explains the validation performed. Finally, conclusions and future work are presented.

2 Background

The background of the work is based on the concepts of software architecture, architectural styles and patterns, non-functional requirements, and expert systems.

2.1 Software Architecture

Software architecture is the fundamental organization of a system embodied in its components, its relationships with each other and with the environment, and the principles that guide its design and evolution [10]. The software architecture offers a set of significant decisions about the organization of a software system, the selection of the structural elements, and the interfaces that make up the system [11].

The software architecture serves as a reference framework to satisfy the requirements, facilitating cost estimation and process management, allowing the analysis of dependencies and consistency of the system [1]. The architectural design allows to definition the behavior that arises from the relationship between the structural elements and their software interfaces, the styles (static and dynamic elements), and architectural patterns, which are used to meet the system requirements and architecture implementation constraints [12].

For this reason, good software architecture is essential both for the design and negotiation of requirements and for establishing discussions between users, developers, and managers [4].

2.2 Architectural Styles

An architectural style is defined as the abstractions of the design patterns, they are the set of restrictions of the functions/characteristics and the relationships of the architectural elements to share functional and structural properties [13]. They not only constrain the architecture but guide the architects during the system development phase [8].

The architectural styles are important and useful during the analysis and design phase of the system, since they provide the guidelines for the construction of the system, indicating the organization and relationship of the components and the manipulation of the data. They allow the architect to determine which style is best suited to the development and which meets its objectives [14]. Some architectural styles are [15]:

- Centralized data: clients access data from a repository.
- Data flow: changes in the successive components of the input data.
- Virtual machines: simulator of functionalities of a software system.
- Call and return: communication between the main program and subprograms through calls.
- Independent components: process communication or independent objects through messages.
- Service orientation: components invoked through interfaces.

2.3 Architectural Patterns

An architectural pattern is the organized structure of software systems in a set of subsystems related to responsibilities, rules, and guidelines; becoming a template for a certain software architecture. The selection of an architectural pattern is a design decision during the development of a system [16].

Architectural patterns focus on a specific problem and context with its limitations and restrictions [17]. The use of architectural patterns helps to understand complex systems, making design limitations visible, since they reuse components and separate elements, providing ease for change and development maintenance [1]. The architectural patterns most used by software architects are presented in Fig. 1.

There are five main architectural patterns [13]: microkernel (when systems have interchangeable components allowing additional features to be added); microservices (they have their own responsibility, can be developed separately and their only dependency is communication); layered architecture (components are organized in interconnected horizontal layers, but not dependent); event-based (they process single-purpose events, from a central unit that sends the data to specialized modules); and space-based (useful for applications with multiple, variable, and unpredictable users by dividing processing and storage across multiple servers).

2.4 Non-functional Requirements

The non-functional requirements are those restrictions to the emergent properties of the system, which are presented according to the needs of the user. They can constrain the system to be developed, as well as the process that must be performed to develop it. It is very common for users to propose non-functional requirements as general goals of the

Fig. 1. Classification of architectural patterns. Source: Own elaboration based on [18].

Table 1. Non-functional requirements.

Non-functional requirements	Description
Availability (reliability)	The ability of the system to remain operational
Scalability	Ability to extend architectural, data, or procedural design
Modifiability	Possibility of making changes to the system
Functionality	Ability to achieve goals
Interoperability (integrality)	Ability to work with other components and/or systems
Integrity	Absence of information alterations
Maintainability	Low-cost modification capability
Portability	Possibility of being executed on different platforms and/or environments (hardware or software)
Reusability	Possibility that the structure or components are implemented in future applications
Security	Resist unauthorized use and denial of service while continuing to offer services to legitimate users
Performance	Execute the operations within the given constraints (time, accuracy, and/or memory usage)
Efficiency	Make proper use of resources such as disk, memory, or processor
Usability	Ease for the user to carry out activities with the system
Testability	Ease of the system showing its failures when tested
Confidentiality	Deny unauthorized access to information
Configurability	Possibility for the user to make changes to the system
Response time	The length of time taken for a system to react to a given event

Source: Own elaboration based on [3, 17, 18].

project, which establish good intentions, but there may be a later interpretation, which is a problem for developers at the time of delivery of the system [19].

Table 1 describes some non-functional requirements that will be the fundamental basis of the proposed expert system.

The non-functional requirements are affected by the architecture, whose impact can be positive or negative, generating advantages or disadvantages between the different architectures [14], which generates a potential conflict between them. For example, performance is improved by the use of coarse-grained components and maintainability by the use of fine-grained components, and if both attributes are needed in the system, a neutral solution should be sought [3].

A key point when analyzing quality attributes is that they cannot be 100% satisfied, since the satisfaction of one attribute can have positive or negative effects on the other attributes, this phenomenon is known as trade off.

2.5 Expert Systems

An expert system (ES) is an application that has information on a knowledge base, from one or more experts to solve problems in a specific area. Expert systems are a means through which knowledge acquired directly or indirectly from domain experts from different scientific areas is shared and distributed. They do not only help for users who lack specific knowledge, but also support or even a substitute for human experts. Therefore, the power of an ES must lie in its ability to imitate the human decision process [20]. The main components of an ES are: the knowledge base, facts, rules, and an inference engine.

The knowledge base is a type of database, which has the ability to make deductions with the stored information since in addition to facts (statements that represent concepts) it has a set of rules that relate the antecedent information with the consequent through of a conditional structure [21].

The facts in a knowledge base make the inference engine obtain automatic deductive reasoning, by combining the information received from the user with the knowledge and relationships available in the knowledge base, selecting the possible rules to give solution to a particular problem and thus obtain information that is not explicit [6].

Expert systems are classified as deterministic or stochastic, depending on the nature of the problems they solve. Deterministic systems are known as "rule-based systems" since they use a logical reasoning mechanism to draw conclusions from those rules. Stochastic systems involve uncertain situations and require methods to measure uncertainty [22].

3 Related Works

Next, some works that address software architecture from the perspective of knowledge-based systems are described.

In [23] an analysis of the impact of change in the evolution of software architectures is carried out. The change propagation process is based on a knowledge-based system that stores the model instances. When a modification is applied, propagation rules are triggered to simulate the impact on the software architecture and its source code.

Among the proposals for the reuse of model-based software architectures are [5], which presents a megamodel that provides a homogeneous means to capture the knowledge of the architecture, making it shareable and reusable; includes a formal mapping of key architecture concepts in order to model artifacts. In [24] a reusable software architectural knowledge model is presented, which helps the architect within the design process to understand the relationship between the different architectural solutions and how they impact the reasoning of the architectural design.

Some works are based on semantic approaches. In [25] a prototype tool is described that queries the architectural knowledge stored in a semantic wiki using SPARQL as query language and answers questions for architectural review, design, and development activities. In [26] a framework is presented that allows the search for software architecture information in the artifacts generated in virtual development communities. It uses an ontology-based semantic search mechanism to retrieve architecture properties and the logic of decisions made during software construction.

There are also approaches for recovering architectural models based on clustering techniques. In [27], the recovery of the architecture is done through the grouping of sets based on three types of dependencies: structural, semantic, and directory. While in [28], an empirical evaluation of a modularity clustering technique used for software architecture recovery is performed.

Among other approaches is [29], which proposes a framework/tool to assist the design of software architecture based on a system of recommendations and oriented to well-known design patterns using contextual factors.

No works similar to the one proposed were found where, through an ES, the selection of a certain architecture can be supported according to the non-functional requirements specified for a software project. The related works described are based on other techniques such as modeling, clustering, semantic techniques, knowledge management, and recommendation systems.

4   Expert System Elaboration Process

To provide a tool that supports decision-making, the expert system ES3A (Expert System for Selection of Software Architecture) was developed.

The ES elaboration process consisted of the following phases. First, the identification of the problem. In this case, the selection of a suitable software architecture for the development of a system from the non-functional requirements of a software development project.

Then, the selection of the target variable and its values, based on a previous bibliographic review and related to architectural patterns and styles. Each of these variables was analyzed and those that did not generate the possibility of interaction were discarded. Satisfied requirements are shown in green, those that can be satisfied depending on the development in yellow, and those that are not satisfied in red. The requirements that are not found in any of the categories (without color), are those that the bibliographic review did not provide any results and can be taken as neutral. Next, a selection of the input variables and their possible values was made. The values of these variables are determined by the indicators shown in Table 2.

Table 2. Indicators

Indicator	A1	A2	A3	A4	A5	A6	A7	A8	A9	A10	A11
Availability											
Efficiency											
Integrity											
Interoperability											
Maintainability											
Portability											
Reusability											
Testability											
Usability											
Scalability											
Modifiability											
Security											
Performance											
Time response											

A1: Layers, A2: Client/Server, A3: Pipes and Filters, A4: Microkernel, A5: Services, A6: Model View Controller, A7: Peer-to-Peer, A8: Components, A9: Centralized Data, A10: Data Flow, A11: Virtual machines. Source: Own elaboration based on [30].

After the non-functional requirements that influence each pattern or architectural style were identified and each was assigned a value. For the user view, the values for each indicator are high, medium, and low, and at the code level, this data is replaced by the numerical values 2, 1, and 0, respectively, depending on whether the impact is positive or negative on the target variable.

Next, the set of rules was designed. For this phase, the elements previously defined in Table 2 were used. Table 3 presents the rules with their antecedent and consequent.

Rule 12 was created to give the architect an alternative to choose the architectural pattern that is most effective for development, in case of not obtaining any results with the previous rules.

Later, the software tool that implements the ES was developed. Three layers were defined for this phase: interface, program logic, and data, so that the interface is independent of the system and that changes in the knowledge base do not alter the programming. The knowledge base and the inferences were carried out in the Prolog language and the design and implementation of the interface were elaborated using the Java programming language. Prolog is a language designed for the representation and processing of knowledge on some subject, the programming is based on clauses that represent facts and rules of the modus ponens type and the execution seeks to satisfy the questions through backward reasoning, deep searches (depth first) and backtracking. Figure 2 presents the components of the ES.

Table 3. Set of rules defined in the expert system

#	Antecedent rule	Consequent
1	D = 2, E = 0, I = 1, In = 1, M = 2, P = 1, R = 1, FP = 2, U = 2, Es = 2, Mo = 1, S = 1 y Re = 2	Layers
2	D = 2, E = 0, I = 0, In = 1, M = 2, P = 2, R = 1, FP = 1, U = 0, Es = 2, Mo = 2, S = 2 y Re = 2	Client/Server
3	D = 1, E = 0, I = 0, In = 2, M = 1, P = 2, R = 2, FP = 2, U = 1, Es = 1, Mo = 2, S = 1 y Re = 2	Pipes and filters
4	D = 2, E = 0, I = 1, In = 2, M = 1, P = 2, R = 2, FP = 2, U = 1, Es = 0, Mo = 1, S = 1 y Re = 2	Microkernel
5	D = 2, E = 0, I = 0, In = 2, M = 2, P = 2, R = 1, FP = 1, U = 2, Es = 2, Mo = 2, S = 2 y Re = 2	Services
6	D = 2, E = 0, I = 1, In = 1, M = 2, P = 1, R = 1, FP = 2, U = 1, Es = 1, Mo = 1, S = 1 y Re = 1	Model View Controller
7	D = 2, E = 2, I = 1, In = 0, M = 0, P = 0, R = 1, FP = 0, U = 0, Es = 2, Mo = 1, S = 0 y Re = 2	Peer to peer
8	D = 2, E = 0, I = 0, In = 2, M = 1, P = 2, R = 2, FP = 2, U = 0, Es = 2, Mo = 2, S = 1 y Re = 1	Components
9	D = 1, E = 0, I = 0, In = 2, M = 1, P = 2, R = 1, FP = 1, U = 1, Es = 2, Mo = 2, S = 1, De = 1 y Re = 1	Centralized data
10	D = 2, E = 0, I = 0, In = 2, M = 2, P = 2, R = 2, FP = 2, U = 1, Es = 1, Mo = 2, S = 1, De = 1 y Re = 1	Dataflow
11	D = 1, E = 0, I = 1, In = 2, M = 0, P = 2, R = 2, FP = 2, U = 0, Es = 1, Mo = 1, S = 1, De = 1 y Re = 1	Virtual machines
12	Add the difference between the data obtained and those found in the knowledge base of each architectural pattern	The numerical value (1–100)

Source: own elaboration.

Fig. 2. Components of the ES3A expert system. Source: own elaboration.

Figure 3(a) shows the graphical user interface that allows the interaction of the SE with the end user or software architect, which offers the user the possibility of assigning a value to each of the input variables. Once the architect has assigned a value to each of the non-functional requirements, the ES uses the inference engine to obtain, through automatic deductive reasoning, a conclusion on the query made with the most appropriate architecture or, if necessary, with percentages of acceptance for each software architecture, see Fig. 3(b).

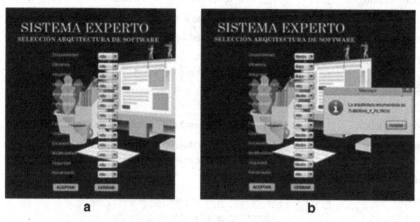

Fig. 3. a. GUI of SE, b. Answer of SE. Fuente: own elaboration.

5 Validation

The developed ES was evaluated by a group of 27 students from a Software Engineering university course. A convenience sample was applied due to the ease of access and availability of the students. The group developed a software project and had to identify a software architecture based on its non-functional requirements. The group used the expert system to perform this task and then filled out a survey with the factors presented in Table 4. These factors were grouped into learning and other aspects that were selected from [31].

Figure 4 shows the results of the learning factors of the ES developed. In general, learning the ES is easy, tasks can be completed, it does not require external help, documentation, or previous experience in expert systems, its language, although technical is adequate and understandable, does not require much learning time, and is easy to understand and learn. Successful completion of tasks (4.7), ease of learning (4.7), and the language used (4.6) stand out with the highest average scores obtained. The factors of documentation, previous experience, and learning time have an inverse evaluation, that is, the lower the values, the better the evaluation.

Figure 5 shows the results of other ES evaluation factors. These factors were evaluated very favorably. 82% of these factors had an average greater than 4.0. The stability of the system and the consistency had the highest values (4.4). Therefore, the ES does not present errors that compromise its stability and presents an adequate integration between its different functions. Other highly valued aspects were ease of navigation (4.1) and reliability. Navigation in the ES is very simple as it consists of a single data

Table 4. Evaluation variables of the expert system.

Variable	Description
Part I. Learning factors	
Ease of learning	It is easy to learn to use the system
Learning time	It took too long to learn how to use the software
Language used	The language used by the system is adequate
Experience in expert systems	To learn to use the system it is necessary to have extensive experience in the use of expert systems
Previous documentation	To use the system it is necessary to read a lot of documentation
Task completion	It is easy to successfully complete a task in the system
External help	It was possible to use the software from start to finish without resorting to outside help
Part II. Other aspects	
Effectiveness	A number of successfully completed tasks
fault tolerance	Identification of errors made by the user
Efficiency	Effort required to achieve a certain goal
Satisfaction	Subjective user satisfaction using the expert system
Scope	Level of correspondence between the system and reality
Suitability	Relationship between the decisions made by the system and users' needs
Reliability	Level of confidence that users have in the decisions made by the system
Consistency	Integrity relationship between system information
Coherence	Ability of the system to reflect reality
Decision quality	Level of understanding of the decisions and their adaptation to the user needs
Response time	Time that the user has to wait from the request to the achievement of a decision
Ease of navigation	Time that the user waits from the request to the achievement of a decision
Screen design	System graphic design
Input and output quality	Quality of the data entry form and the results window
system stability	The system is stable and has no errors

Source: own elaboration.

entry input window and a results report window. Respondents stated that they trust the results delivered and the different architectures identified. The aspect that did not obtain

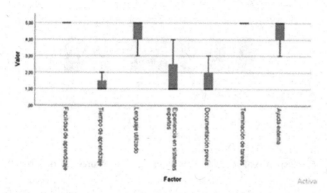

Fig. 4. Evaluation of learning factors. Source: own elaboration.

a high rating was the input and output quality (3.3) because the windows present plain text and require a better visual design.

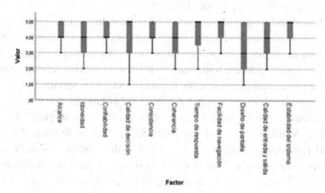

Fig. 5. Evaluation of other factors. Source: own elaboration.

Additionally, the ES was presented to a group of three professional web application developers, to know their perception. For the experts to know how it works and the results delivered, the system was demonstrated with some examples, later they were allowed to test with inputs and validate what was delivered as a recommendation. To know the perception of developers about the system, a more general survey was designed aimed at capturing the perception and interest generated by the proposal, more from the daily professional activity, than from the academic component, this obviated the need to know the theory of expert systems. The results obtained are presented, in percentage, in Fig. 6. The evaluated variables of efficacy, completeness, correctness, understanding, novelty, adequacy, and recommendation were taken from [31].

According to the validation, the path followed by the system is consistent with the actions carried out by an expert in order to make the architectural decision.

Respuestas profesionales %

■ Totalmente en desacuerdo   ■ En desacuerdo
▫ Ni de acuerdo ni en desacuerdo   ■ De acuerdo
■ Totalmente de acuerdo

Fig. 6. Response of professionals by categories. Source: own elaboration.

6 Discussion

Software architecture should highlight the elements and their relationships in a software product. The structure of these elements will be based on the non-functional requirements of the product. Architecture definition is an essential activity that allows reasoning about its properties early in the development lifecycle.

The literature presents a wide spectrum of architectures that does not facilitate an adequate selection according to the needs of a software project. Extensive experience in project development and architecture design and implementation is required. In addition, the selection of an appropriate architecture will allow organizing the system to provide the functional services and guarantee the required quality of service [32].

The ES developed through a non-functional requirements entry form allows generating recommendations on the selection of an architecture adjusted to the requirements identified. Validation tests showed that ES is easy to learn and use. Although non-functional requirements are expressed briefly, they are well-known terms in the Software Engineering domain. Therefore, users do not require much documentation to use the ES. The ES was favorably evaluated in other aspects such as its consistency, stability, and coherence. The quality of the recommended decision is also highlighted. The main aspect to improve is its GUI since the response screen can be presented with a visual aesthetic that facilitates the understanding of the recommended architectures and includes an overview of the process used to reach these conclusions.

On the other hand, non-functional software requirements specify quality attributes. In most cases, it is impossible to maximize all of these attributes. Therefore, the software architect must consider trade-offs, balancing attributes, and considering various alternative architectures. The definition of the software architecture of a product is becoming a fundamental task within the development process, where it is difficult for software professionals to structure the knowledge necessary to identify an adequate architecture, which leads to loss of knowledge. Time, and errors and risks in the projects. The developed expert system is oriented to support this activity that requires relevant knowledge expressed in a set of rules.

For the professionals consulted, the most favorable characteristics are the novelty, efficiency, correctness, and understandability of the ES, which would lead them to recommend it for use in real environments.

7 Conclusions and Future Work

The objective of this work was the development of an expert system that supports the decision-making of a software architect when defining the pattern or architectural style that must be implemented for a software development project. The ES3A expert system developed and based on a set of rules that are used by the inference engine provides recommendations on the type of architecture that can be used according to the values of the non-functional requirements of the product to be built.

The added value of the expert system is obtained as the system becomes more complex. For this initial prototype, the rules have been simplified, but it is expected that the inputs will be more detailed and that chaining will be used. Provided by the inference mechanism, to make the recommendation.

Future work includes adding new facts and rules to the knowledge base; query the values of variables when selecting a certain pattern or architectural style, and include new rules that allow defining the relevance of the non-functional requirements so that they are the starting point of the system.

References

1. Garlan, D.: Software architecture: a travelogue. In: Future of Software Engineering Proceedings, pp. 29–39 (2014)
2. Bosch, J.: Design and use of industrial software architectures. In: Proceedings Technology of Object-Oriented Languages and Systems, TOOLS 29 (Cat. No.PR00275), p. 404 (1999). https://doi.org/10.1109/TOOLS.1999.779093
3. Sommerville, I.: Ingeniería de Software, 9a edn., Pearson Education, México (2011)
4. Hasselbring, W.: Software architecture: past, present, future. In: Gruhn, V., Striemer, R. (eds.) The Essence of Software Engineering. Springer, Cham (2018). https://doi.org/10.1007/978-3-319-73897-0_10
5. Perovich, D., Bastarrica, M.C.: Model-based formalization of software architecture knowledge. In: 2014 IEEE/IFIP Conference on Software Architecture, pp. 235–238. IEEE (2014)
6. Abu Ghali, M.J., Mukhaimer, M.N., Abu Yousef, M.K., Abu Naser, S.S.: Expert system for problems of teeth and gums. Int. J. Eng. Inform. Syst. 1(4), 198–206 (2017)
7. Liebowitz, J. (ed.): The Handbook of Applied Expert Systems. CRC Press, USA (2019)
8. Van Vliet, H., Tang, A.: Decision making in software architecture. J. Syst. Softw. 117, 638–644 (2016).
9. Venters, C., et al.: Software sustainability: research and practice from a software architecture viewpoint. J. Syst. Softw. 138, 174–188 (2018). https://doi.org/10.1016/j.jss.2017.12.026
10. IEEE 1471-2000: IEEE Recommended Practice for Architectural Description for Software-Intensive Systems (2000). https://standards.ieee.org/ieee/1471/2187/
11. Jaiswal, M.: Software architecture and software design. Int. Res. J. Eng. Technol. 2452–2454 (2019)
12. Woods, E.: Software architecture in a changing world. IEEE Softw. 33(6), 94–97 (2016)
13. Richards, M.: Software Architecture Patterns. O'Reilly Media, Incorporated, USA (2015)
14. Kumar, A.: Software architecture styles: a survey. Int. J. Comput. Appl. 87(9), 5–9 (2014)
15. Sharma, A., Kumar, M., Agarwal, S.: A complete survey on software architectural styles and patterns. Procedia Comput. Sci. 70, 16–28 (2015)

16. Schmidt, D.C., Stal, M., Rohnert, H., Buschmann, F.: Pattern-Oriented Software Architecture, Patterns for Concurrent and Networked Objects. Wiley, England (2013)
17. Pressman, R.S., Maxim, B.R.: Software Engineering: A Practitioner's Approach. McGraw Hill, USA (2016)
18. Bass, L., Clements, P., Kazman, R.: Software Architecture in Practice, 3rd edn. Addison-Wesley Professional, Boston, USA (2012)
19. Glinz, M.: On non-functional requirements. In: 15th IEEE International Requirements Engineering Conference (RE 2007), pp. 21–26. IEEE (2007)
20. Saibene, A., Assale, M., Giltri, M.: Expert systems: definitions, advantages and issues in medical field applications. Expert Syst. Appl. 177(March), 114900 (2021). https://doi.org/10.1016/j.eswa.2021.114900
21. Castillo, E., Gutierrez, J.M., Hadi, A.S.: Expert Systems and Probabilistic Network Models. Springer Science & Business Media, New York, USA (2012)
22. Sahin, S., Tolun, R.: Expert System with applications. Int. J. Elsevier 39(4), 4609–4617 (2012)
23. Hassan, M.O., Deruelle, L., Basson, H.: A knowledge-based system for change impact analysis on software architecture. In: 2010 Fourth International Conference on Research Challenges in Information Science (RCIS), pp. 545–556. IEEE (2010)
24. Soliman, M., Riebisch, M.: Modeling the interactions between decisions within software architecture knowledge. In: Avgeriou, P., Zdun, U. (eds.) ECSA 2014. LNCS, vol. 8627, pp. 33–40. Springer, Cham (2014). https://doi.org/10.1007/978-3-319-09970-5_3
25. De Graaf, K.A., Tang, A., Liang, P., Khalili, A.: Querying software architecture knowledge as linked open data. In: 2017 IEEE International Conference on Software Architecture Workshops (ICSAW), pp. 272–277. IEEE (2017)
26. Figueiredo, A.M.C., dos Reis, J. C., Rodrigues, M.A.: Semantic search for software architecture knowledge: a proposal for virtual communities environment. In International Conference on Information Society (i-Society 2011), pp. 270–274. IEEE (2011)
27. Puchala, S.P.R., Chhabra, J.K., Rathee, A.: Ensemble clustering based approach for software architecture recovery. Int. J. Inf. Technol. 1–7 (2021). https://doi.org/10.1007/s41870-021-00846-0
28. Sözer, H.: Evaluating the effectiveness of multi-level greedy modularity clustering for software architecture recovery. In: Bures, T., Duchien, L., Inverardi, P. (eds.) Software Architecture. ECSA 2019. LNCS, vol. 11681. Springer, Cham (2019). https://doi.org/10.1007/978-3-030-29983-5_5
29. Sielis, G.A., Tzanavari, A., Papadopoulos, G.A.: A social creativity support tool enhanced by recommendation algorithms: the case of software architecture design. In: Kunifuji, S., Papadopoulos, G., Skulimowski, A., Kacprzyk , J. (eds.) Knowledge, Information and Creativity Support Systems. Advances in Intelligent Systems and Computing, vol. 416. Springer, Cham (2016). https://doi.org/10.1007/978-3-319-27478-2_34
30. Suárez, J.M., Gutiérrez, L.E.: Tipificación de dominios de requerimientos para la aplicación de patrones arquitectónicos. Información tecnológica 27(4), 193–202 (2016)
31. Miranda, P., Isaias, P., Crisóstomo, M.: Evaluation of expert systems: the application of a reference model to the usability parameter. In: Stephanidis, C. (ed.) UAHCI 2011. LNCS, vol. 6765, pp. 100–109. Springer, Heidelberg (2011). https://doi.org/10.1007/978-3-642-21672-5_12
32. Oquendo, F., Leite, J., Batista, T.: Software Architecture in Action. Springer International Publishing, Cham (2016). https://doi.org/10.1007/978-3-319-44339-3

Gamified Strategies to Increase Motivation in Middle School Programming Learning: A Systematic Mapping

Andrés Felipe Rodríguez González$^{(\boxtimes)}$, María Clara Gómez Álvarez ,
Gabriel Mauricio Ramírez , and Bell Manrique Losada

Universidad de Medellín, Cra 87 N 30-65, Medellín, Antioquia, Colombia
{afrodriguez,mcgomez,gramirez,bmanrique}@udemedellin.edu.co

Abstract. Digital transformation is one of the main problems facing Colombia, the lack of students interested in starting studies in university programs associated with Computer Science is one of the leading causes of this problem. Currently, worldwide and in Colombia, there is a deficit of professionals associated with these areas of science. Therefore, identifying the reasons for the low demand of students in these programs is important when the labor demand is so high. Based on this, a systematic mapping was carried out to identify the gamification strategies used to increase the levels of interest and motivation in programming in middle school students who are about to start their university program. The mapping was based on 652 initial papers, of which 19 were accepted as they met all the inclusion and quality criteria and had sufficient in-formation to answer the research questions. It was found that the most used technological strategies are associated with video games, robotics, and the practice-based learning technique. Most of the methodologies are complemented with gamification elements, demonstrating their usefulness in increasing student interest.

Keywords: Motivation · School · Gamification · Computational thinking · Programming

1 Introduction

Digital development in the modern era brings, as a consequence, new needs and technological changes associated with technological evolution per se. It makes necessary to maintain a constant innovation and renewal of processes that, at the time, did not have technological support for their realization, generating delays in time and high human incidence. To maintain a stable demand for technological renewal in the world, it is necessary to have more human capital interested in computer science [1].

Unfortunately, in recent years the demand has been outstripping supply worldwide. In 2017, more than 7000 vacancies related to technological areas were reported in Colombia, and they were not filled due to the lack of human capital [2]. The trend seems to be increasing, as it is projected that by 2025 the deficit of only programmers in the Colombian market will reach more than 110,000 [3].

V. Agredo-Delgado et al. (Eds.): CCC 2022, CCIS 1775, pp. 87–101, 2023.
https://doi.org/10.1007/978-3-031-36357-3_7

According to the trend, several economic sectors in Colombia could likely enter crisis due to the technological lag concerning the global reality [4]. To slightly mitigate this problem, the Colombian national government proposes providing free programming training to 50,000 people over 15 years of age who are interested in the area [5]. However, this number will not be enough to cover the country's needs in the short term.

Considering the above scenario and looking for sustaining the complete training cycle, by according to the international standards defining Computer Science, it is essential to know why the number of students graduating in the area does not meet the actual demands [6]. Several researchers justify the problem of students' lack of motivation and frustration in the complexity of learning programming [7]. They also mention the following causes: (i) the high level of attrition in new students of Computer Science [8], (ii) the lack of clarity of students for understanding what Computer Science is and what their role as professionals will be [9]; and (iii) generating false and unrealistic expectations [10].

Because of the above, it is essential to know the approach of the curricula design of the technological subjects from middle-school education. At this educational level and how the principles of Computer Science are approached [11, 12] is an essential factor in guiding the life projects of students so that they are encouraged and interested in continuing its learning path in Computer Science.

This paper aims to perform a systematic mapping focused to gamified strategies applied in middle-school institutions to increase interest and motivation in learning programming in students, seeking to increase the percentage of students potentially interested in to begin a Computer Science career.

The paper is organized as follows: the first sections are associated with the problem context, followed by general and specific objectives. Subsequently, the systematic mapping associated with the research topic; finally, we describe the conclusions and the proposed future work.

2   Methodology

A systematic mapping study is the process of identifying, categorizing, and analyzing existing literature that is relevant to a certain research topic. In this paper, the systematic mapping presented was performed following the methodology proposed by Petersen [13] and it's detailed in Fig. 1.

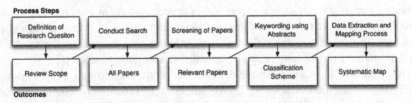

Fig. 1. Methodology steps. Image taken from: [13]

From the problem mentioned in the previous section, the following pre-question is posed: What are technological gamification strategies used to increase motivation for programming in middle school education?

Within the framework of the reference methodology, the subsequent elements were defined in the process to be followed: research objectives, research questions, keywords, databases, search chains of the databases, criteria for inclusion and exclusion of papers, results obtained after applying the criteria, analysis of data and results and, finally, answers to the research questions.

The management process of the systematic mapping process was supported on the online tool Parsifal. The analysis processes were developed by using the VOSviewer and Jasp-Stats tools.

2.1 Goals

The general goal of the systematic mapping is analyzing the technological strategies based on gamification, which have been used to increase the interest levels of high-school students in continuing their professional studies in Computer Science.

The specific goals proposed are the following:

- Comparing the tools used to implement the strategies proposed.
- Finding programming teaching patterns applied within the approaches examined.
- Classifying the strategies analyzed according to the place of application and their social environment.
- Highlighting the levels of effectiveness in the execution of the gamified technological strategies.

2.2 Research Questions

Considering the problem's description and goals, the research questions proposed for the systematic mapping were:

- Q1: What strategies have been proposed to increase the level of motivation in programming in middle-school students?
- Q2: What methodologies have been used to measure the level of student motivation in programming?

2.3 Keywords

The keywords defined for the systematic mapping are the following:

- Words in spanish: Educación Media, Pensamiento Computacional, Gamificación, Motivación, y Programación.
- Words in English: Secondary School, Computational Thinking, Gamification, Motivation, and Programming.

2.4 Databases

ACM, Dimensions EBSCO, Science Direct, and SCOPUS are the databases defined and used to perform the systematic mapping information search.

2.5 Query Search

The query search used in the databases is presented below. It is essential to clarify that the syntax was applied to all databases.

(("Colegios" OR "Educación Media" OR "Secondary School" OR "High School" OR "Middle School") AND ("Motivación" OR "Motivation" OR "Interest") AND ("Gamificación" OR "Gamification") AND ("Learning" OR "Aprendizaje") AND ABS ("Programación" OR "Programming" OR "Coding") AND NOT ("primary school" OR "escuela") AND NOT TITLE ("university" OR "universidad" OR "Higher education") AND NOT TITLE ("e-learning") AND NOT ("AI" OR "IA")) AND (PUBYEAR > 2016).

2.6 Inclusion and Exclusion Criteria

The inclusion and exclusion criteria proposed in the systematic mapping were managed using the Parsifal tool to complement the systematic mapping process. The criteria are as follows:

- Inclusion criteria: Papers written in Spanish and English; papers mentioning technological environments, results of the effectiveness of strategies, gamification, teaching programming, and secondary education; and papers published between 2017–2021.
- Exclusion criteria: Papers with approaches applied to primary-school, high-schools, and university institutions but without methodology elements, the topics are not related to programming, E-Learning or MOOC approach, a paper written in other languages, scope does not contribute to the research and papers published before 2016.

2.7 Search Process

Once the information search was performed in the selected databases for developing the mapping, the inclusion and exclusion criteria were applied.

A general review was carried out in which duplicate papers were identified; subsequently, the titles, abstracts, and conclusions of each document were reviewed to identify the papers that answered the research questions.

In the search process, we omitted papers focused to higher education institutions or knowledge areas different from Computer Science. The results obtained are presented in the Sect. 3.

The PICOC features (population, intervention, comparison, results, and context) of the systematic review are as follows:

- Population: Students
- Intervention: Gamification
- Comparison: Strategies
- Outcomes: Learning, Interest
- Context: Schools, Colleges, Middle school

3 Results

In this Section we present the main findings of the systematic mapping in relation with gamification strategies to increase motivation in computer programming learning at middle schools.

In the research process, once the inclusion and exclusion criteria were applied, we obtained 652 papers in the five databases, as we show in the Table 1.

Table 1. Results of the systematic review.

ACM	Dimensions	EBSCO	Science Direct	SCOPUS	Total
160	57	148	174	113	652

From the 652 papers selected, 41 ones were accepted according to the quality criteria, corresponding to the 6.3%, and distributed in each database (see Fig. 2). It is important to note that when a paper met an exclusion criterion, it was rejected; however, all the inclusion criteria had to be met to be accepted.

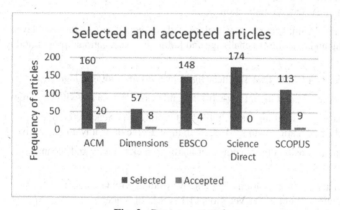

Fig. 2. Papers accepted.

Following Petersen's methodology, a score was assigned to each accepted paper according to the quality evaluation metrics proposed for the review, such as: the proposal uses gamification, describes a technological strategy, it's applied in middle school institutions, it's based on programming area, contributes to increase the interest and motivation of students, and proposes effective evaluation methodologies. Each paper proposal was be rated with an integer value between zero (0) and two (2). In this sense, we define six metrics, allowing a maximum score of twelve (12) to be assigned to a paper—the minimum cut-off score required for the paper to be approved is eight (8). In Table 2 we show the score obtained by each accepted paper.

Table 2. Scores of papers initially accepted

#	Name of the paper	Score
1	A comparative study of gamification in programming education in a Croatian high school	11
2	A Serious Game for Learning C Programming Language Concepts Using Solo Taxonomy	8
3	A systematic review on open educational games for programming learning and teaching	7
4	A visual programming environment for introducing distributed computing to secondary education	9
5	An affective and Web 3.0-based learning environment for a programming language	5
6	Analyzing students' experience in programming with computational thinking through competitive, physical, and tactile games: the quadrilateral method approach	5
7	Battling gender stereotypes: A user study of a code-learning game, "Code Combat," with middle school children	10
8	C++ adventure: A mixed methods pilot study on digital game-based learning of coding and effect on motivation	12
9	Can typical game features have unintended consequences? A study of players' learning and reactions to challenge and failure in an educational programming game	12
10	Code Lab: A Game That Teaches High Level Programming Languages	11
11	Code Notes: Designing a Low-Cost Tangible Coding Tool for/with Children	9
12	Computational thinking and robotics: A teaching experience in compulsory secondary education with students with high degree of apathy and demotivation	12
13	Creating and using digital games for learning in elementary and secondary education	7
14	Design and Implementation of Interactive Coding with Gamification for Web Programming Subject for Vocational High School Students	12
15	Developing problem solving competency using functional programming style	8
16	EasyPAP: A framework for learning parallel programming	7
17	Evaluating Aspects of Usability in Video Game-Based Programming Learning Platforms	5
18	Evaluation of Game Templates to Support Programming Activities in Schools	9
19	Executable Examples for Programming Problem Comprehension	6
20	Game design-based learning of programming	6
21	Gamification based mobile application as learning media innovation for basic programming lessons	10
22	Gamification-Based Learning Media in Object-Oriented Programming Subjects to Increase Learning Motivation of VHS Students	0

(*continued*)

Table 2. (*continued*)

#	Name of the paper	Score
23	Gamifying the first programming class: Outcomes and antecedents of continued engagement intention	0
24	Genius Learning Strategy of Basic Programming in an Adventure Game	7
25	Implementing Flipped Classroom Strategy in Learning Programming	7
26	Improving 7th-graders' computational thinking skills through unplugged programming activities: A study on the influence of multiple factors	7
27	Learning Programming by Creating Games through the Use of Structured Activities in Secondary Education in Greece	9
28	Make world, a collaborative platform to develop computational thinking and STEAM	7
29	One mobile application for the development of programming skills of secondary school students	8
30	Reducing Caribbean's Students' "Code-Phobia" with Programming in Scratch	0
31	sCool - Game Based Learning in STEM Education: A Case Study in Secondary Education	8
32	Students learning performance and perceived motivation in gamified flipped-class instruction	6
33	Syntax Exercises in CS1	6
34	Teacher Perspectives on Introducing Programming Constructs through Coding Mobile-Based Games to Secondary School Students	3
35	Teaching How to Program Using Automated Assessment and Functional Glossy Games (Experience Report)	7
36	Teaching of programming - An educational performance booster for students at economically disadvantaged schools	2
37	Teaching Principles of Programming without ICT: Sharing Experiences on the Design of a Board Game	8
38	The effect of coding teaching on students' self-efficacy perceptions of technology and design courses	7
39	Transitioning from introductory block-based and text-based environments to professional programming languages in high school computer science classrooms	9
40	Turing Project: An Open Educational Game to Teach and Learn Programming Logic	6
41	Using an Online Serious Game to Teach Basic Programming Concepts and Facilitate Gameful Experiences for High School Students	11

3.1 Data Analysis and Results

According to the acceptance criteria associated with the quality metrics, of the 41 accepted papers, only 19 final papers in the systematic mapping met the quality acceptance criteria, *i.e.*, 2.9% of the total number of papers selected and 46.3% of the total number of papers accepted.

Most of the papers accepted were from the Scopus database, which had a 42% acceptance rate of selected papers; on the other hand, no papers were accepted from Dimensions. The accepted papers are recorded in Table 3.

Table 3. Papers accepted.

#	Name of the paper	Authors
1	C++ adventure: A mixed methods pilot study on digital game-based learning of coding and effect on motivation	Cu Hao, L. and Delantar, M.B. and Tan, G.J
2	Using an Online Serious Game to Teach Basic Programming Concepts and Facilitate Gameful Experiences for High School Students	Montes, H. and Hijon-Neira, R. and Perez-Marin, D. and Montes, S
3	Can typical game features have unintended consequences? A study of players' learning and reactions to challenge and failure in an educational programming game	Chase, C.C. and Malkiewich, L.J. and Lee, A. and Slater, S. and Choi, A. and Xing, C
4	A comparative study of gamification in programming education in a Croatian high school	Schatten, M. and Schatten, M
5	Gamification based mobile application as learning media innovation for basic programming lessons	Hidayat, W.N. and Fitranti, A. and Firdaus, A.F. and Kartikasari, C.D.I. and Sutikno, T.A
6	sCool - Game Based Learning in STEM Education: A Case Study in Secondary Education	Steinmaurer, A. and Pirker, J. and Gütl, C
7	Design and Implementation of Interactive Coding with Gamification for Web Programming Subject for Vocational High School Students	Arif, R.F. and Rosyid, H.A. and Utomo, P
8	Computational thinking and robotics: A teaching experience in compulsory secondary education with students with high degree of apathy and demotivation	Díaz-Lauzurica, B. and Moreno-Salinas, D

(continued)

Table 3. (*continued*)

#	Name of the paper	Authors
9	Code Notes: Designing a Low-Cost Tangible Coding Tool for/with Children	Sabuncuoğlu, Alpay Erkaya, Merve Buruk, Oğuz Turan Goksun, Tilbe
10	Teaching Principles of Programming without ICT: Sharing Experiences on the Design of A Board Game	Uribe, Nitae A.O Ortiz, Ariel O.B Casanova, Pedro E.N
11	Battling gender stereotypes: A user study of a code-learning game, "Code Combat," with middle school children	Yücel, Yeliz Rizvanoglu, Kerem
12	One mobile application for the development of programming skills of secondary school students	Salahli, M. A Yildirim, E. et al
13	Transitioning from introductory block-based and text-based environments to professional programming languages in high school computer science classrooms	Weintrop, D Wilensky, Uri
14	A visual programming environment for introducing distributed computing to secondary education	Broll, Brian Lédeczi, Ákos et al
15	Code Lab: A Game That Teaches High Level Programming Languages	White, Robert Tian, Feng Smith, Peter
16	Learning Programming by Creating Games through the Use of Structured Activities in Secondary Education in Greece	Seralidou, Eleni Douligeris, Christos
17	Developing problem solving competency using functional programming style	Mollov, Muharem Petrov, Petar
18	A Serious Game for Learning C Programming Language Concepts Using Solo Taxonomy	Yassine, Alaeeddine Chenouni, Driss Berrada, Mohammed Tahiri, Ahmed
19	Evaluation of Game Templates to Support Programming Activities in Schools	Schindler, Christian Slany, Wolfgang Beltrán-Jaunsarás, et al

To present the results of the mapping more clearly, descriptive data on the papers reviewed are shown in Table 4.

According to Table 4, the most accepted papers are between 2020 and 2021; which current research topic is recent and is being worked on. In addition, the majority of the 147 rejected papers, were between 2019 and 2021. However, this indicates that, although

Table 4. Distribution of accepted, duplicate, and rejected papers by year.

Status	Year	Frequency	Percent
Accepted	2016	1	2.439
	2017	5	12.195
	2018	8	19.512
	2019	8	19.512
	2020	8	19.512
	2021	10	24.390
	2022	1	2.439
	Missing	0	0.000
	Total	41	100.000
Duplicated	Total	32	100.000
Rejected	2016	0	0.000
	2017	79	13.644
	2018	79	13.644
	2019	114	19.689
	2020	134	23.143
	2021	130	22.453
	2022	43	7.427
	Missing	0	0.000
	Total	579	100.000

the papers referenced the research problem, they did not cover it entirely. The problem is also given special attention in other settings such as universities or elementary schools.

As seen in Table 5, most papers were rejected for having a university approach in their content or they not generating an essential value to the research applied in schools. On the other hand, most of the accepted papers focused on middle-school institutions or topics associated with programming.

In addition, within the accepted papers, in Fig. 3 we show a clustering among the keywords included.

Based on Fig. 3, we can precise: (i) the keywords are the nodes, and the relationships are the arcs of the cluster; (ii) the colors are associated with the proximity among topics (*e.g.,* programming subjects, games subjects); (iii) we can't identify an evident correlation among the authors of the papers. In Fig. 4 we present the existing clustering; it should be clarified that there are only relationships between the authors of each paper.

The lack of correlation among authors may be due to the few papers selected and the fact that all papers were written within three last years, making it difficult to cite each other. In addition, the publication of these papers was likely simultaneous or very close to each other.

Table 5. Distribution of accepted and rejected items according to selection criteria.

Status	Selection Criteria	Frequency
Accepted	About technological environments	1
	Does not add value to research	0
	Focus on e-learning or MOOC	0
	Focus on elementary schools	0
	Focus on universities	0
	It is not written in Spanish or English language	0
	Not an article	0
	Use gamification	2
	Topic not related to programming	0
	Topic related to programming	38
	Missing	0
	Total	41
Rejected	About technological environments	0
	Does not add value to research	98
	Focus on e-learning or MOOC	16
	Focus on elementary schools	10
	Focus on universities	49
	It is not written in Spanish or English language	7
	Not an article	44
	Use gamification	0
	Topic not related to programming	355
	Topic related to programming	0
	Missing	0
	Total	579

The selected papers highlight the application of methodologies around the world, considering the social and academic conditions of the environment. The strategies were applied to students between 11 and 16 years old.

It is essential to highlight that in countries such as Philippines, the analyzed proposals were focused on the different technical emphasis of the students. The measurement variables and contents differ according to the knowledge level in basic programming.

On the other hand, different programming languages are used to carry out the strategies, with a 21% of Python (4/19 papers) as the predominant one. However, due to the age of some students, it is worth clarifying that in other strategies do not use programming languages but pseudocode or block-based code (4/19 papers by using Scratch).

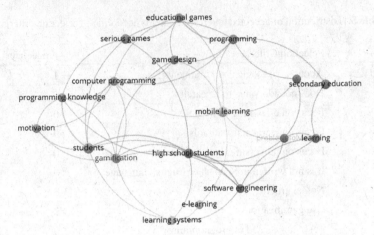

Fig. 3. Clustering between keywords of selected papers.

In most cases, it is necessary to have a computer for applying the strategies because of the tools used are web-based or desktop-based applications. Even so, strategies oriented to mobile devices and even robots are presented. It is important to note that the two papers do not present effective results given that their objective was present a new tool and describe its use.

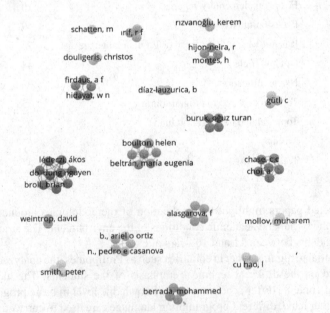

Fig. 4. Clustering among authors of selected papers

In summary, the relevant data obtained are presented below:

- Country of application: Philippines, Ecuador, United States, Croatia, Indonesia, Australia, Spain, and United States
- Target population: Students from 11 to 16 years old
- Technological tools used: Mobile devices, Computer, and Robots
- Gamification elements used: Rewards, competition, achievements, levels, and scoring
- Effectiveness measurement elements: Pre-test and post-test surveys, situational motivation scale, computer emotional scale
- Programming language taught: C++, C, Python, Javascript, Block-based code, and Pseudocode.

3.2 Answers to the Questions

Considering the above results and all the conditions to the review process, we answer the research questions:

RQ1: ¿What strategies have been proposed to increase the level of motivation in programming in middle school students? The strategies used to increase motivation in programming in middle school students are mainly based on a) Video games (7 papers – 36%); b) block programming (4 papers – 19%); c) mobile/web applications (5 papers – 26%); d) disconnected activities, which are performed without the support of technological devices (2 papers); and e) robotics (1 paper). Gamification plays a fundamental role in motivating students and is the pillar of the proposed strategies. The usage of scores, competitions, and rewards allows students to focus on understanding, executing, and learning in a didactic way.

RQ2: ¿What strategies have been proposed to increase the level of motivation in programming in middle school students? The methodologies that have been used to measure motivation and interest of students, are as follows: (a) surveys, which consist in a series of questions before and after the execution of the strategy, in order to know the changes in the students' perceptions after their participation; (b) situational motivation scale, which is designed to assess aspects of intrinsic motivation, identified regulation, external regulation and demotivation [14], adapted for a specific academic environment; (c) computerized emotional scale, an artifact allowing to evaluate emotions (*e.g.,* anger, anxiety, joy, and sadness) during computer-based learning [15]. Although the models for measuring student motivation in the process of learning programming were found to be successful, it is worth noting that only 11 papers presented statistical or model-based evidence of this measurement. In the other papers, motivation was not measured; however, they supported their claims on direct observation of the students and on what, in the researchers' opinion, perceived attitudinal changes in them.

4   Conclusions and Future Work

The research questions posed for this systematic mapping are satisfactorily answered. It is essential to recognize gamification as one of the most appropriate tools to increase students' interest in programming.

Although gamification is often related to games, it is essential to differentiate and understand the concepts. Applying gamification to other types of strategies is possible. In this systematic mapping, it was possible to find gamified strategies associated with video games and robotics. However, exploiting other fields more accessible to all educational institutions in any socioeconomic context is recommended, considering limitations in physical and technological infrastructure.

It is essential to expand this systematic mapping to learn about other strategies used to increase students' interest in the programming area, according to age and educational level. The competences level of each group under study should be considered, and, and specific methodologies by according their characteristics should be determined, that really make them feel motivated.

The identification of effectiveness measures for the strategies should continue studied. Although pre and post-test surveys are suitable methods, it is possible to look for methodologies that can be applied in parallel with the strategy to observe the progress of the students.

References

1. Spieler, B., Grandl, M., Ebner, M., Slany, W.: Bridging the gap: a computer science pre-MOOC for first semester students. Electron. J. e-Learn. **18**(3), 248–260 (2020)
2. Ministerio de las Tecnologías de la Información y las Comunicaciones – MINTIC. Estudio de la brecha de talento digital (2018)
3. MinTIC. Ministerio TIC ofrecerá oportunidades de empleo a estudiantes de Misión TIC 2022, anunció la ministra Karen Abudinen (2020). https://mintic.gov.co/portal/inicio/Sala-de-pre nsa/Noticias/160664:Ministerio-TIC-ofrecera-oportunidades-de-empleo-a-estudiantes-de-Mision-TIC-2022-anuncio-la-ministra-Karen-Abudinen. Accessed 11 Feb 2022
4. Ulloa, G.: ¿Qué pasa con la ingeniería en Colombia? (2008). https://eduteka.icesi.edu.co/art iculos/IngenieriaColombia. Accessed 5 Feb 2022
5. ¡Aprenda programación en 2022! Gobierno amplió fecha de inscripciones para que 50 mil colombianos se capaciten en el lenguaje del siglo XXI. https://mintic.gov.co/portal/inicio/ Sala-de-prensa/Noticias/195459:Aprenda-programacion-en-2022-Gobierno-amplio-fecha-de-inscripciones-para-que-50-mil-colombianos-se-capaciten-en-el-lenguaje-del-siglo-XXI. Accessed 16 Feb 2022
6. En Colombia faltan 80.000 ingenieros informáticos | Sociedad Colombiana de Ingenieros. https://sci.org.co/en-colombia-faltan-80-000-ingenieros-informaticos/. Accessed 16 Feb 2022
7. Figueiredo, J., Lopes, N., García-Peñalvo, F.J., García, F.: Predicting Student Failure in an Introductory Programming Course with Multiple Back-Propagation (2019). https://doi.org/ 10.1145/3362789.3362925
8. Raigoza, J.: A study of students' progress through introductory Computer Science programming courses. In: Proceedings - Frontiers in Education Conference, FIE, vol. 2017-Octob, pp. 1–7 (2017). https://doi.org/10.1109/FIE.2017.8190559
9. Grover, S., Pea, R., Cooper, S.: Remedying misperceptions of computer science among middle school students. In: SIGCSE 2014 – Proceedings of the 45th ACM Technical Symposium on Computer Science Education, pp. 343–348 (2014). https://doi.org/10.1145/2538862.253 8934
10. Luxton-Reilly, A.: Learning to Program is Easy (2016). https://doi.org/10.1145/2899415.289 9432

11. Flórez, F.B., Casallas, R., Hernández, M., Reyes, A., Restrepo, S., Danies, G.: Changing ag way of thinking: teaching computational thinking through programming. Rev. Educ. Res. **87**(4), 834–860 (2017). https://doi.org/10.3102/0034654317710096

12. Maltese, A.V., Tai, R.H.: Pipeline persistence: examining the association of educational experiences with earned degrees in STEM among U.S. students. Sci. Educ. **95**(5), 877–907 (2011). https://doi.org/10.1002/sce.20441

13. Petersen, K., Vakkalanka, S., Kuzniarz, L.: Guidelines for conducting systematic mapping studies in software engineering: an update. Inf. Softw. Technol. **64**, 1–18 (2015). https://doi. org/10.1016/j.infsof.2015.03.007

14. Guay, F., Vallerand, R.J., Blanchard, C.: On the assessment of situational intrinsic and extrinsic motivation: the Situational Motivation Scale (SIMS). Motiv Emot **24**(3), 175–213 (2000). https://doi.org/10.1023/A:1005614228250

15. Kay, R.H., Loverock, S.: Assessing emotions related to learning new software: the computer emotion scale. Comput Human Behav **24**(4), 1605–1623 (2008). https://doi.org/10.1016/j. chb.2007.06.002

Google Cloud Vision and Its Application in Image Processing Using a Raspberry Pi

Santiago Valencia Saavedra[✉] and Ana Lorena Uribe

Universidad Nacional de Colombia, Sede Manizales Kilómetro 7 vía al Magdalena, Manizales, Caldas, Colombia

{savalenciasa,alhurtadou}@unal.edu.co

Abstract. This document aims to highlight the advantages of using the optical character recognition (OCR) software provided by Google Cloud Vision and how it can be effectively used with a Raspberry Pi, a small platform with limited processing and memory capabilities. OCR involves the conversion of images containing text into machine-encoded text that can be easily processed by computers. It is a computationally intensive task that requires significant processing power and memory, which can be a challenge for smaller platforms like the Raspberry Pi. However, by utilizing the Google Cloud Vision platform, we can remotely perform OCR requests, allowing us to offload the processing load to Google's powerful servers. This results in significant performance improvements, making it possible to achieve high accuracy rates in OCR tasks. In our experiment, we processed 19 images of Colombian vehicle license plates using the Google Cloud Vision platform through a Raspberry Pi. Our tests showed that the OCR accuracy rate was 100%, demonstrating the effectiveness of this approach. Furthermore, the use of a Raspberry Pi can help reduce hardware costs, as it is an affordable platform that can be easily configured and connected to a network. This makes it an attractive option for small businesses or individuals who need to perform OCR tasks but do not have the resources to invest in high-end hardware.

Keywords: Google Cloud Vision · optical character recognition · image processing · Raspberry Pi

1 Introduction

Computers using artificial intelligence algorithms allow to interpret the information contained in digital images, one of the techniques used by artificial intelligence to perform image processing is computer vision. Computer vision allows to automate some tasks that the human visual system can perform. The most common tasks performed by automatic computer vision systems allow processing, analyzing, recognizing objects, and extracting textual information from digitized images [1], see Fig. 1 (taken from [2]) shows a general representative model of the components of a computer vision analysis system.

V. Agredo-Delgado et al. (Eds.): CCC 2022, CCIS 1775, pp. 102–113, 2023.
https://doi.org/10.1007/978-3-031-36357-3_8

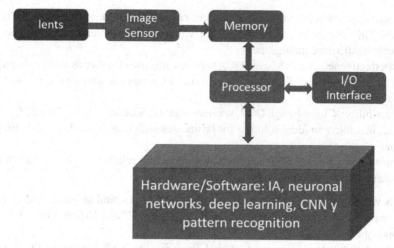

Fig. 1. Computer vision system architecture

The model of Fig. 1 shows a sensor that captures images, coupled to a machine that has memory and a processor with an input/output interface which, in turn, has software/hardware installed or configured for executing the image processing.

Cloud computing and optical character recognition (OCR) are two rapidly growing technologies that have revolutionized the way we process and store information. Cloud computing refers to the delivery of computing services, including servers, storage, databases, software, and networking, over the internet. On the other hand, OCR is a technology that enables machines to read the printed or handwritten text and convert it into digital data. Combining these two technologies has resulted in significant advancements in data processing and management.

According to [3] and [4], there are several OCR services available on the internet. Some of the popular one is cloud-based include:

- Google Cloud Vision OCR: Google Cloud Vision OCR is a cloud-based OCR service that uses Google's machine learning technology to extract text from images.
- Microsoft Azure OCR: Microsoft Azure OCR is a cloud-based OCR service that provides accurate and reliable text extraction from images [5]
- Amazon Textract: Amazon Textract is a cloud-based OCR service that uses machine learning to extract text from scanned documents [6].

On the other heads, Cloud-based OCR has several benefits over traditional OCR systems[1]. Some of these benefits include:

–

---

[1] https://www.klippa.com/en/blog/information/on-premise-ocr/.

Scalability: Cloud-based OCR services can scale up or down based on the user's needs. This allows users to handle large volumes of documents without worrying about infrastructure management.
- Cost-effectiveness: Cloud-based OCR services are cost-effective as users only pay for the resources they use. This eliminates the need for expensive hardware and software installations.
- Accessibility: Cloud-based OCR services can be accessed from anywhere in the world, making it an ideal solution for businesses with remote workers or distributed teams.
- Security: Cloud-based OCR services are secure and reliable, as they are hosted on secure servers with redundant backups.

This work presents a prototype human-machine interaction model to identify text found on photographs of license plates using the Google Cloud Vision API (GCV) and a Raspberry Pi 4.

When it comes to integrating Google Cloud Vision with a Raspberry Pi, there are a few different ways to approach it. One common method is to use the Google Cloud Vision API, which allows developers to send image files to the Cloud Vision service for processing and receive the results in pseudo-real time.

Making an analogy with Fig. 1, the sensor used in this model is a generic webcam, connected to a Raspberry Pi version 4 (hardware) with operating system Raspbian version 11 (software) to which the GCV client and the connectivity credentials required by the platform have been installed so that through the communications network it connects with the GCV server software, that is responsible for processing the image using optical character recognition (OCR) techniques. The GCV server software returns to the Raspberry the text found in the images sent. Afterward, with the received text, local processing is performed to simulate if the license plate has access to a specific area.

2 Implementation

One of the primary benefits of using cloud computing for OCR is that it allows for faster processing and analysis of data. OCR technology has been around for several decades, but it was limited by the processing power of the machines it was running on. With cloud computing, OCR algorithms can be run on powerful servers, which can process data at a much faster rate. This has resulted in increased efficiency and productivity for businesses and organizations that rely on OCR technology.

Another benefit of using cloud computing for OCR is that it enables real-time collaboration and data sharing. In the past, OCR was limited to local machines, which made it difficult to share data across different locations. However, with cloud computing, data can be stored and accessed from anywhere in the world, allowing for seamless collaboration and data sharing between different teams and departments.

Additionally, cloud computing provides a more secure and reliable way of storing and processing data. Cloud providers typically have robust security measures in place to protect against data breaches and cyber-attacks. This means that data processed using OCR technology is less susceptible to security breaches, ensuring the safety and confidentiality of sensitive information.

Despite the numerous benefits of using cloud computing for OCR, there are also several challenges associated with this technology. One of the primary challenges is the cost of implementing and maintaining cloud infrastructure. Cloud computing requires significant investment in hardware, software, and infrastructure, which can be a significant expense for small and medium-sized businesses.

Another challenge associated with cloud computing and OCR is data privacy and compliance. When processing and storing sensitive data in the cloud, organizations must ensure that they comply with data privacy regulations such as General Data Protection Regulation (GDPR) and Health Insurance Portability and Accountability Act (HIPAA). Failure to comply with these regulations can result in severe penalties and legal consequences.

Lastly, cloud computing and OCR require significant technical expertise to implement and maintain. Organizations must have skilled IT professionals to manage and optimize their cloud infrastructure and OCR algorithms. This can be a challenge for organizations that do not have the necessary resources or expert.

According to [7], one branch of artificial intelligence is computer vision, which seeks to understand the content of digital images through the implementation of computational algorithms as defined by [8].

In agreement with [9], the functionality of OCR software is to extract the information contained in an image and convert it into text. Subsequently, when the text is extracted from the image, a cleaning process is performed to extract the data required by the application to be implemented.

"At the core of such systems there are three fundamental principles: Integrity, Intentionality, Adaptability. The principle of integrity defines that the observed object must be considered as a "whole" consisting of many interrelated parts. The principle of intentionality assumes that any interpretation of the data must be useful for some purpose. Finally, the principle of adaptability implies that the application developed must be capable of self-learning."[2]

In the development of this project, we applied the principles of integrity and intentionality. We send the image as it was taken by the camera to the GCV API and when the characters contained in the image are received, we feed a prototype software that simulates the access of cars to a specific area, determining if the license plate is allowed or not in the system.

---

[2] https://pdf.abbyy.com/es/learning-center/what-is-ocr/.

Our code organizes the data returned by the OCR - GCV API to allow car accesses but does not perform any learning process.

The computational code base of the client software connects to the GCV API was taken from https://cloud.google.com/vision/docs/ocr.

3 Specifications of the System

Figure 2 presents a flow diagram of the main components of the system.

- Image capture: this process is responsible for receiving the main input variable, which is the path to the directory where the image of interest to be processed (vehicle license plate) is stored. The image to be processed by the system is obtained from the related directory; this must be a single image containing the license plate.
- Transmission of the image to the GCV classification system: there are four sub-processes in this block: extraction of text from the plate image, reception of the processed strings, local processing of the strings, and access verification.

  - Extraction of text from the image of the plate: this is the sub-process that is in charge of invoking the API for image processing, with the plate captured by the sensor, the image is sent to the remote GCV platform.
  - Reception of the processed strings: the text of the image returned by the application is obtained as an array data structure with four fields. The first field contains the letters, the second field the numbers, the third field a dash and the last field the city to which the vehicle belongs. The software only validates the first two fields of the array to allow vehicle access.
  - Local processing of the strings received: this sub-process opens and reads the file containing the list of authorized plates. It oversees verifying if the text received from the GVC software is in this file. If the comparison returns a valid value, access to the vehicle containing the license plate is allowed.
  - Access verification: the system output shows, in text mode, the final decision taken by the system, i.e., whether the processed plate is granted access.

The client code implemented in this project was written in the Python programming language and executed from the Raspberry Pi, the details of the connection and the processing of the text received by the GCV are presented in Program 1.

Line 4 presents the connection instructions from the client code to the GCV platform.

Line 12 presents the instructions that load the image to the client application.

Line 15 allows sending the image to the GCV platform to be processed by the OCR software.

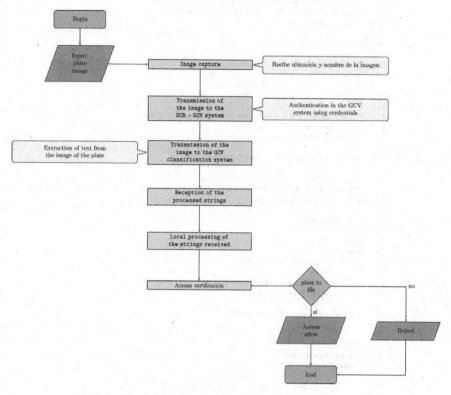

Fig. 2. Flowchart of the system functionality

Line 17 captures the text returned by the server.

Line 53 performs the local verification of the received text.

Lines 26–38 print the accuracy with which the text identification is done. Finally, the program prints the elapsed time between sending the image to be processed and receiving the GCV API response.

```
1. import time
2. import os,sys
3. """Communication with Google Cloud Vision API credentials."""
4. os.environ['GOOGLE_APPLICATION_CREDENTIALS']
   r"object_detection.json"
5.
6. def detect_text(path):
7.
8.    from google.cloud import vision_v1 as vision
9.    import io
10.   client = vision.ImageAnnotatorClient()
11.
12.
13.   """Open the image that is in the path that enters in the function"""
14.   with io.open(path, 'rb') as image_file:
15.      content = image_file.read()
16.
17.   image = vision.types.Image(content=content)
18.
19.   response = client.text_detection(image=image)
20.   """Receive the texts extracted from the image"""
21.   texts = response.text_annotations
22.
23.   start = time.time();
24.   infile = 0
25.   plateE = []
26.   print(path)
27.   """Processing cycle to receive text"""
28.   for text in texts:
29.      """Stores each of the text strings in the image in an array."""
30.      plateE.append(text.description)
31.
32.      print("\n"{}'".format(text.description))
33.
34.
35.   """Handles error"""
36.   if response.error.message:
37.      raise Exception(
38.         '{}\nFor more info on error messages, check: '
39.         'https://cloud.google.com/apis/design/errors'.format(
40.            response.error.message))
41.   end = time.time()-start
42.
43.   """Local processing of the received strings according to length for later comparison
      with the data stored in the text file because some plates are identified with a dash -
      """
44.
45.   if len(plateE) == 4 and plateE[2] != '-':
46.      plateAr = plateE[1] +" "+ plateE[2]
47.   elif plateE[2] != '-':
48.      plateAr = plateE[1] +" "+ plateE[2]
49.   else:
50.      plateAr = plateE[1] +" "+ plateE[3]
51.
52.   """Opening of the file containing the enabled plates"""
53.   with open("/home/pi/Desktop/object_detection/placas","r") as file1:
54.      """Compare each line of the plate file with the plate entered in the image."""
55.      for line in file1:
56.         if line[0:7] == plateAr:
57.            infile = 1
58.   print('time: {}'.format(end))
59.   """If it finds the plate, it enables access, otherwise it denies it."""
60.   if infile == 1:
61.      print('PLATE: {}'.format(plateAr)+' ACCESS ')
62.   else:
63.      print('PLATE: {}'.format(plateAr)+' DENY')
64.
65. path = sys.argv[1]
66. detect_text(path)
```

4 Experimental Framework and Results

4.1 The System Architecture

In the following, we present the infrastructure and software utilized for implementing Google Cloud Vision and OCR. Our goal is to provide a comprehensive overview of the tools and technologies that were employed to enable these powerful image recognition capabilities. By leveraging cutting-edge infrastructure and advanced software solutions, we have been able to achieve highly accurate and efficient results in our image-processing tasks. In this article, we will delve into the specific details of our implementation, including the hardware and software components used, as well as the specific algorithms and techniques employed to achieve our objectives. Overall, our hope is that this information will prove valuable to other professionals and organizations seeking to implement similar image recognition solutions.

The developed model architecture is shown in Fig. 3. The architecture is implemented with a Raspberry Pi 4 model B with 4GB of RAM, a Cortex-A72 processor and a 16 GB SD storage memory. The Raspberry has connected a keyboard, a monitor, a mouse, and a Genius Face Cam 1000X High Definition 720 horizontal lines webcam with an image resolution of 1280×720 pixels.

The operating system installed on the Raspberry Pi is Raspbian version 11; Python 2.7 version, the GCV client, and connectivity credentials provided by the GCV server must also be installed on the Raspberry Pi to allow the remote OCR software execution.

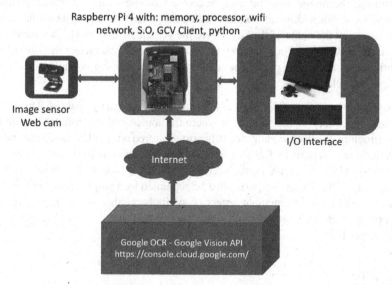

Fig. 3. Model project architecture

For the correct execution and communication of the client code on the Raspberry with the Google API, the following installations were carried out: GCV client on the Raspberry, the generation of the API credentials file given by the Google Cloud platform which must be invoked from the source code and the repository of the images of the plates to be processed.

5 Data Sets

According to the Colombian Ministry of Transportation, there are different types of license plates[3].

For the implementation of this work, those defined as passengers were selected: private, commercial, official, and old cars.

A proprietary data set was created with 19 plates. The list of processed plates is shown in Table 1. Additionally, photos of plates extracted from different web pages are selected.

A local repository is created where the images of the Colombian car plates are stored. The objective is to have an initial set of these images in a specific location for the application to obtain and process them. The specifications of the images are defined as follows:

- Name: a unique name is generated for each plate for its classification plus the extension of the image file (e.g. plate1.jpeg).
- Location: the images of the plates are in a single location that functions as a repository of images to be sorted. This repository is in Raspberry's local storage as a directory in the same path where the source code that performs the image processing is located.
- Condition: the image must be a capture of a Colombian license plate (yellow), it must not contain additional text to the license plate, which has six alpha-numeric characters and the name of the city where the vehicle is registered. This format must be guaranteed since the code identifies the alphanumeric characters that are the main identifiers of the license plate. The image must be a drawing containing the license plate of the vehicle.

The text file contains only the list of license plates that will be enabled. This file is in the general repository, in the same path where the source code is stored. This file has a specific structure, the license plates identification is stored one per line in the file and must be structured in two parts as follows: the first part corresponds to the first three letters of the license plate, e.g. (AAA); the second part corresponds to the three identifying numbers, e.g. (123). These two parts must be separated by a single space between them and there must be no intermediate letters or symbols, neither at the beginning nor at the end of the plate structure. Accordingly, each line of the file should be readable as follows: AAA 123.

6 Results

Table 1 shows the accuracy and total processing times returned by the GCV OCR platform.

---

[3] https://es.wikipedia.org/wiki/Anexo:Matriculas_automovilisticas_de_Colombia.

Table 1. Accuracy and elapsed times of plate processing on GCV platform.

Plate	Accuracy	Elapsed Times (ms)
JBS703	1	0,000756
CAN732	1	0,001090
XZF607	1	0,000601
ODV947	1	0,002010
AID899	1	0,000546
AAA123	1	0,001711
BSI859	1	0,000558
QGU210	1	0,000569
QFO640	1	0,000602
CZR263	1	0,000667
RMT679	1	0,000719
FAC579	1	0,001894
UEU308	1	0,003492
KGZ445	1	0,001791
QGU210	1	0,000575
EPM633	1	0,000938
JBS835	1	0,002003
HNK167	1	0,000643
GTN326	1	0,001689

As can be observed in the second field of Table 1, the platform returns with an accuracy of 100% the alphanumeric characters contained in the processed images. The response times of the GCV platform are acceptable for this type of program where it is required to quickly give a set of vehicles access to a given area. Although the Raspberry is a computer with limited computational components, using such remote platforms as GCV allows an application to perform fast processing.

7 Conclusions and Future Work

In the initial review of the API, it was made clear that it has multiple applications for image recognition. For the purposes of this work we used the detection of text within an image and applied this API module to recognize license plates.

An accuracy of 100% was obtained after processing 19 plate images using the GCV API and GCV's OCR software.

Once the operating system has been installed and updated on the Raspberry Pi 4 and the GCV credentials have been integrated, it is evident that the software only runs correctly with the 2.7 version of Python. With Python 3.0 version there is a conflict generated with the packages imported from GCV, specifically the" vision_v1" package.

The integration of cloud computing with GCV and OCR has revolutionized data processing and management. By leveraging the power of cloud computing, OCR can now offer faster data processing, real-time analysis, and seamless data sharing, while also improving data security and reliability. However, implementing this technology can pose challenges such as high costs for setup and maintenance, data privacy concerns, and the need for specialized technical expertise. Additionally, services like GCV may incur processing fees. Therefore, before adopting these technologies, organizations must assess their needs and resources carefully, and implement suitable measures to overcome these challenges. With careful planning and execution, cloud computing and OCR can transform data management and provide a competitive edge to organizations.

In conclusion, the combination of Google Cloud Vision and a Raspberry Pi provides an effective solution for OCR tasks, allowing users to achieve high accuracy rates without needing expensive hardware upgrades.

8 Future Work

Cloud-based OCR services have a wide range of applications across different industries. In the healthcare industry, OCR technology can be used to convert patient records and medical documents into digital format, allowing healthcare professionals to access and share patient information more efficiently. In the financial industry, OCR technology can be used to process large volumes of financial documents, such as invoices and receipts, quickly and accurately.

In the legal industry, OCR technology can be used to convert paper-based legal documents into digital format, making them easier to search and retrieve.}

We propose as future work to test different types of free OCR software like Open CV in order to compare the accuracy and elapsed times presented in this paper with the OCR - GCV software.

References

1. Vaithiyanathan, D., Muniraj, M.: Cloud based text extraction using google cloud vison for visually impaired applications. In: 2019 11th International Conference on Advanced Computing (ICoAC) (2019)
2. Sugadev, M., Yogesh, Sanghamreddy, P.K., Samineni, S.K.: Rough Terrain Autonomous Vehicle Control Using Google Cloud Vision API. IEEE Xplore (2020)
3. Bansal, S., Gupta, M., Tyagi, A.K.: A necessary review on Optical Character Recognition (OCR) system for vehicular applications. In: 2020 Second International Conference on Inventive Research in Computing Applications (ICIRCA) (2020)
4. Chen, F., Wang, C.: Image recognition technology based on cloud computing platform. J. Intell. Fuzzy Syst. 39(4), 5119–5129 (2020)
5. Onyejegbu, L., Ikechukwu, O.: Optical character recognition as a cloud service in azure architecture. Int. J. Comput. Appl. 146(13), 14–20 (2016). https://doi.org/10.5120/ijca20169 10898

6. Hegghammer, T.: OCR with Tesseract, amazon textract, and google document AI: a benchmarking experiment. J. Comput. Soc. Sci. 1–22 (2021). https://doi.org/10.1007/s42001-021-00149-1

7. Mangold, S., Steiner, C., Friedmann, M., Fleischer, J.: Vision-based screw head detection for automated disassembly for remanufacturing. Procedia CIRP **105**, 1–6 (2022). https://doi.org/10.1016/j.procir.2022.02.001

8. Pachipala, Y., Nandhitha, E., Haritha, K., Chandrika, B., Jadala, V.C.: Face recognition application using offloading computation over google cloud. In: 2022 6th International Conference on Computing Methodologies and Communication (ICCMC) (2022)

9. Cabanillas-Carbonell, M., Chávez, A.A., Barrientos, J.B.: Glasses connected to google vision that inform blind people about what is in front of them. In: 2020 International Conference on e-Health and Bioengineering (EHB) (2020)

Human Development for the Brave: Supporting the Generation of Empathy, Work in Development

Juan Camilo Useche[1]($\boxtimes$), Pablo Figueroa[1], and Leonardo Parra-Agudelo[2]

[1] Departamento de Ingeniería de Sistemas y Computación,
Universidad de los Andes, Bogotá, Colombia
{jc.useche10,pfiguero}@uniandes.edu.co
[2] Departamento de Diseño, Universidad de los Andes, Bogotá, Colombia
leonardo.parra@uniandes.edu.co

Abstract. The project seeks to support the generation of empathy that can be created through 360 virtual reality videos. Empathy is understood as the ability to understand and respond appropriately to the thoughts and feelings of other people. To support the creation of empathy, a virtual reality application is being developed in which 360 videos can be viewed. Using this application, different functionalities are being explored that can contribute to the generation of empathy. Functionalities are being introduced and will be validated in experiments with users to improve them and find new opportunities for improvement. At the end of the project, it is expected to have identified the contribution that some functionalities and elements can have in the generation of empathy. It is expected that this project will serve as motivation for future research exploring the potential of virtual reality as a tool for empathy generation. The progress of the project is presented.

Keywords: Empathy · Virtual Reality · 360° Videos

1 Introduction

Virtual reality has been used by multiple organizations as a means of generating empathy. Empathy is understood as the ability to understand and respond appropriately to the thoughts and feelings of other people. These organizations create experiences around situations that require wills and actions from the community. This is achieved by showing users stories with a realism that other media do not offer and that bring people closer to the situations, so that it is difficult to be indifferent.

In the literature there are different participation mechanisms that can be integrated into an experience that have not been exhaustively explored in virtual reality and the generation of empathy, to the best of our knowledge. This has motivated us to explore the implementation of these functionalities in a virtual reality application and to understand the role they can play in relation to empathy generation. This application will show users 360 videos and introduce functionalities and elements that could contribute to

V. Agredo-Delgado et al. (Eds.): CCC 2022, CCIS 1775, pp. 114–121, 2023.
https://doi.org/10.1007/978-3-031-36357-3_9

the generation of empathy. The project has made some advances in a bullet comments functionality for annotations on the 360 videos. The other functionalities considered will not be shown implemented in this article. The research will focus on the behavioral component of empathy. This component refers to acting to help others by understanding their situation and feelings.

2 Objectives

The objective of the project is to identify the contribution of functionalities and elements to the generation of empathy. For this purpose, a virtual reality application is developed to which different functionalities and elements can be introduced. The virtual reality application allows the visualization of 360 videos that seek to generate empathy and introduces the functionalities and elements around the content of these videos. This in order to support the generation of empathy that can be created through 360 virtual reality videos.

3 Related Work and References

As mentioned previously, there are different applications and 360 videos that make use of virtual reality to generate empathy. Likewise, there are a variety of authors who have proposed functionalities and elements that could contribute to the generation of empathy. The most relevant projects are discussed around the following topics: empathy and virtual reality, bullet comments and test questions associated with videos. The results of greatest value for the application of the present project are gathered.

3.1 Empathy and Virtual Reality

One of the projects of relevance to the investigation uses as its basis the virtual reality video published by the New York Times in 2015, The Displaced [1]. The video explores the lives of three children who were displaced from their homes by wars and persecution. The video offers a window into the lives of these children. They talk about how they escaped from war zones, memories of their homes and their hopes for the future. It is an experience that portrays the impacts of war and displacement on these children. This is done with an immersive realism that generates a strange sense of connection with people whose lives are far away. This project has been recognized with awards that acknowledge its value, such as the Grand Prix - Lions Entertainment (Entertainment Branded Content & Visual Storytelling Innovation in Visual Storytelling and Branded Entertainment) at Cannes Lions'16, or "The Most Next Award", the highest award of the annual AICP Next awards of the Association of Independent Commercial Producers, among other awards.

In 2017, Sundar et al. [2] conducted a study analyzing the effectiveness of virtual reality in generating empathy by making use of the project developed by the New York Times, The Displaced [1]. The methodology used consisted of dividing users into three groups where each group experienced the stories through a different medium (VR, Video-360 and text). Participants completed a questionnaire at the end of reading or watching each story. Some of the metrics used to measure the effectiveness of the experience were the following:

Dispositional Empathy. Using the Interpersonal Reactivity Index [3].

Standard Literature Measurements of Presence. [4] to measure immersion.

Empathy was assessed using Batson's adjective empathy scale [5]. At the end of the procedures, it was found that participants who experienced the stories through VR or Video-360 were more empathetic towards the characters than those who only read the text based on the stories. The emotional intensity of the story was also found to be a key factor in the effectiveness of the experience. Virtual reality technologies have the potential to be applicable to multiple contexts and expose stories that can represent different groups. On the other hand, [2] suggests different scales that can be used to measure the empathy generated by the developed application. Likewise, [6] analyzes 26 publications on tools to generate empathy in order to develop a framework to design this type of tools. The article provides techniques to measure the efficiency of a tool to generate empathy. These techniques will be useful in the design of the evaluation of the application.

Virtual reality is a tool that is being used in classrooms for educational purposes [7]. Philippe Bertrand has studied virtual reality as a tool to generate empathy [8] and was able to work on a project where he brought virtual reality into a classroom. Bertrand suggests that discussion around 360 video content should be encouraged. Users tend to demonstrate self-declared empathy towards the subjects of the video, as long as important details of the experience are highlighted to them, and they actively participate in a discussion about the content and the concepts of the empathy phenomena themselves as applied to their daily lives. The functionalities implemented for the virtual reality application will help highlight important details of the experience and encourage discussion around the content presented in the video.

3.2 Bullet Comments

Bullet comments are comments that are displayed on a video and are associated with a timestamp. The use of these comments has proven to bring benefits in terms of video content understanding, perceived engagement and social connection between individuals [9]. [10] proposed and investigated an implementation of bullet comments in 360 videos, which served as a reference for the development of this application. Among the results of the study are comments from participants that reference the concept of empathy. The effect of these comments in generating empathy is something that, to the best of our knowledge, has not been explored and has great potential for impact on the virtual reality application being developed in the project. Therefore, bullet comments are one of the participation mechanisms that will be explored in the application. Emphasis is placed on the effect of these in the generation of empathy.

3.3 Test Questions Associated with the Videos

Another functionality valuable for the implementation of the application is the use of test questions associated with the videos. The use of test questions embedded in a video [11] has been investigated in order to mitigate the lack of feedback to the user in traditional lectures and videos. It was found that these questions are effective when seeking to generate content that enhances participation and interaction, which helps in formative processes. It is important to take into account the motivation with which a user approaches the questions (completeness, challenge-seeking, feedback or review) in order to design the questions accordingly. The generation of empathy is a formative process for which these questions can be applied and which, to the best of our knowledge, has not been explored.

4 Application Design

4.1 Theme and Synopsis

Through this application, the user can visualize and intervene 360 videos that seek to generate empathy.

4.2 Functionalities

Before watching a video in the application, the user is presented with a series of questions about the contents of the video. While watching the video, the user can make annotations through bullet comments to help him/her answer the questions posed at the beginning. After watching the video a first time, the user can watch the video again in another viewing mode in which he/she can see the comments that other users have left.

4.3 Functionalities and Empathy

The preliminary questions presented to the user are expected to motivate the user to use the annotation functionality. The content of the questions should provoke the user to reflect on what he/she is seeing in the video, which is expected to contribute to the generation of empathy. Another way to support empathy generation is by highlighting important details about the video content. The annotation functionality will allow users to highlight the details they consider important and discover those that other users considered important. On the other hand, the people who generated the videos, the authors of the stories, will be able to observe the annotations left by users and will be able to analyze the thoughts and emotions of those who watched their videos. It is expected that this reflection will generate empathy in the authors of the video towards the users and that this will help to improve the production of future content.

5 Implementation

5.1 Technology Involved

The application was developed in Unity 2020.3.1f1 and an Oculus Quest 2 was used for its development. The OVR plugin (ver. 1.70.0) that provides tools for the development of Oculus VR applications was used. From the OVR plugin we mainly used the OVR Camera Rig that makes use of a 3D model to show the Oculus controllers to the user. This so that it was easy to map the functionalities to different buttons and to aid the user in case he/she does not know which button to press.

5.2 Experience Flow

Figure 1 shows a collection of images illustrating the functionalities of the application.

Fig. 1. The functionalities present in the application a) current application mode in the user control label, b) player leaving a comment at a point in the video and holding the trigger to increase its duration, c) icon that appears in front of the user when the video is paused, d) display of the comments icon, which indicates that there are comments available in the area, e) multiple comments left at the same point during the "view comments" mode.

Fig. 2. Illustration of annotations in a 360 video: the user views the video through a virtual reality device and points with the controller to display the comments.

Before starting the application, the user is presented with questions to be answered at the end of the video. These questions are related to the content of the video and are intended to motivate the user to use the bullet comments functionality to answer them.

When starting the application, the 360 video is played. The application has two modes, "leave comments" and "view comments", the current mode can be verified by checking the label that appears on the left control (A, Fig. 1). The application starts in the "leave comments" mode, while the application is in this mode all the comments already existing in the video (left by other users) are hidden and the user can start leaving the comments needed to answer the questions. To make the comments be associated to a segment of the video, the user must hold down the right control index trigger pointing to the area where they want to leave a comment (Fig. 3). While the trigger is pressed, a marker will appear over the area where the comment will be left and a label will appear on the right control showing the time captured until the user releases the trigger (B, Fig. 1). The captured time will indicate the duration of the comment (how long it remains active) on the video when entering the "view comments" mode (Fig. 2). The user can, after finishing watching the videos, use the comments left in the "leave comments" mode (these are not deactivated at any time) to answer the questions posed at the beginning. The comments left by the user in the "leave comments" mode are not disabled at any time. The user can use these comments to answer the questions posed at the beginning, once he/she has finished watching the video. On the other hand, comments left by users will be saved in a database to ensure persistence and allow future users to view the comments of past users.

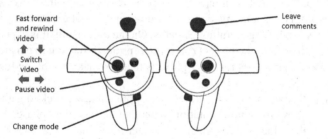

Fig. 3. Mapping of controls to application functionalities

While in "leave comment" mode, the user has control over the current time of the video. He can stop, fast forward or rewind it at his convenience. The time control functionalities are accessed by using the left joystick control and the main X button. Pressing the X button stops or resumes the video, the joystick moves to the right or left to fast forward or rewind the video, respectively. An icon will appear in front of the user to indicate the current status of the video (C, Fig. 1).

Pressing the hand trigger on the left-hand control will take the user into the "view comments" mode. The button can be pressed again to toggle between the two modes. In the "view comments" mode the user can view comments left by other users in different time segments and in different areas of the video. While in this mode the user cannot leave any comments, however, the user can hover the pointer over one of the available comments to view the comments associated with that zone. When a comment is available in the zone a comment icon will appear (D, Fig. 1). Placing the pointer over the icon shows the user a drop-down list of comments associated with that zone. If multiple users left a comment in that zone, the drop-down list shows them all (E, Fig. 1). If there are no active comments in the zone the comment icon disappears as long as there are no active comments.

It is expected to conduct a first experiment with the application developed for which a group of users who will use the application will be gathered. Before starting the experiment, they will be given an initial questionnaire to find out about their previous knowledge of virtual reality applications and to measure their empathy with an index. At the beginning of the experiment, they will be given a list of questions about the content of the video that they will have to answer once they finish watching it. They will have to use the functionality to leave comments as a tool to answer these questions. After answering the questions, the video will be played again. This time, they will be able to observe the comments left by other users. In order not to introduce a bias associated with which comments users see, it is planned to use the wizard of oz method to generate the comments left by other users. After the experiment is over, they will be asked to fill out a final questionnaire to get feedback on the application's functionalities and measure a new empathy index.

6 Future Work

At the end of the project, it is expected to have identified the contribution that some functionalities and elements can have in the generation of empathy. It is expected that this project will serve as a motivation for future research that explores the potential of virtual reality as a tool for generating empathy. On the other hand, it is expected that the application resulting from the project can support projects that aim to generate empathy in people and serve as a basis for other projects that can make use of the functionalities introduced.

With the first experiment on the developed application, we seek to gather feedback from users to improve the implementation in another development phase. A next development phase will include the introduction of other functionalities and elements such as test questions embedded in videos.

At the end of the project, the project can be validated by comparing its performance against a conventional annotation tool. A conventional annotation tool can consist of viewing the 360 videos on a platform such as YouTube and making the annotations in a comment forum.

Acknowledgements. The author would like to acknowledge Jairo Carrillo and Paula Barriga for their work on the Human Development for Brave project, the UNDP Project Acceleration Office and the University of La Guajira for their continued collaboration with the project.

References

1. Silverstein. J.: The Displaced: Introduction. The New York Times Magazine (2021). https://www.nytimes.com/2015/11/08/magazine/the-dis-placed-introduction.html. Accessed Dec 2.
2. Sundar, S.S., et al.: Being there in the midst of the story: how immersive journalism affects our perceptions and cognitions. Cyberpsychol. Behav. Soc. Network. **20**(11), 672–682 (2017). https://doi.org/10.1089/cyber.2017.0271

3. Davis, M.H.: A multidimensional approach to individual differences in empathy. JSAS Catalog Select. Docum. Psychol. **10**, 85 (1980)
4. Baños, R.M., Botella, C., Garcia-Palacios, A., et al.: Presence and reality judgment in virtual environments: a unitary construct? Cyberpsychol. Behav. **3**, 327–335 (2000). https://doi.org/10.1089/10949310050078760
5. Batson, C.D., Sager, K., Garst, E., et al.: Is empathy-induced helping due to self–other merging? J. Pers. Soc. Psychol. **73**, 495–509 (1997). https://doi.org/10.1037/0022-3514.73.3.495
6. Pratte, S., Tang, A., Oehlberg, L.: Evoking empathy: a framework for describing empathy tools. In: Proceedings of the Fifteenth International Conference on Tangible, Embedded, and Embodied Interaction (TEI 2021). Association for Computing Machinery, New York, NY, USA, Article 25, 1–15 (2021). https://doi.org/10.1145/3430524.3440644
7. Fatma, K.: How Virtual Reality is Being Used in Curriculum to Develop Empathy. Nov 14, 2019 (2021). https://higheredconnects.com/virtual-reality-to-develop-empathy/. Accessed Dec 3
8. Bertrand, P., Guegan, J., Robieux, L., McCall, C., Zenasni, F.: Learning empathy through virtual reality: multiple strategies for training empathy-related abilities using body ownership illusions in embodied virtual reality. Front. AI Robot. **5**, 28 (2018). https://doi.org/10.3389/frobt.2018.00026
9. Lee, Y.-C., Lin, W.-C., Cherng, F.-Y., Wang, H.-C., Sung, C.-Y., King, J.-T.: Using time-anchored peer comments to enhance social interaction in online educational videos. In: Proceedings of the 33rd Annual ACM Conference on Human Factors in Computing Systems, pp. 689–698 (2015). https://doi.org/10.1145/2702123.2702349
10. Li, Y.-J., Shi, J., Zhang, F.-L., Wang, M.: Bullet comments for 360°Video. In: 2022 IEEE Conference on Virtual Reality and 3D User Interfaces (VR), pp. 1–10 (2022). https://doi.org/10.1109/VR51125.2022.00017
11. Cummins, S., Beresford, A., Rice, A.: Investigating engagement with in-video quiz questions in a programming course. IEEE Trans. Learn. Technol. **9**, 1 (2015). https://doi.org/10.1109/TLT.2015.2444374

Model for the Evaluation of the Quality of Open Data

Monica Rosa Lopez-Guayasamin$^{(\boxtimes)}$ and Nestor Dario Duque-Mendez

Universidad Nacional de Colombia, Sede Manizales, Manizales, Colombia
{mrlopez,ndduqueme}@unal.edu.co

Abstract. In Colombia, Law 1712 of 2014 "Transparency and Access to Information", defines open data as all primary or raw data, found in standard and interoperable formats that facilitate access and reuse, which are under the custody of public or private entities that fulfill public functions and that are made available to any citizen, freely and without restrictions, so that third parties can reuse them and create services derived from them.

In the Open Data policy, the central issue is the Quality of the same. Although there are several approaches and definitions on the subject, there is no single integrated model with specific metrics to be able to objectively evaluate the characteristics involved in quality. This article proposes to identify the relevant characteristics in the quality of open data, define metrics for its evaluation and automatic and/or semi-automatic mechanisms for its calculation.

Keywords: Open Data · Data Quality · Quality Metrics

1 Introduction

In April 2018, the national government approved the CONPES 3920 document that defines the data exploitation policy (Big Data) for the Colombian State. With this document, the country assumes regional leadership by being the first in Latin America, and eighth in the world, with a comprehensive public policy that enables the use of data to generate social and economic development [1]. This policy motivates the promotion of public access to information, and the significant increase in timely and reliable data.

The Open Data government policy defined by MINTIC [2] reference the following guidelines:

- Trusted digital services
- Secure and efficient internal processes based on IT capabilities
- Data-driven decision making
- Empowerment of the citizen through the consolidation of an open state
- Boosting the development of smart territories and cities

One of the high-impact factors in the implementation of this policy is the quality of the data, which represents a problem that is affecting the different sectors of the market: commercial, official, industrial, educational, among others. The lack of data quality in

V. Agredo-Delgado et al. (Eds.): CCC 2022, CCIS 1775, pp. 122–135, 2023.
https://doi.org/10.1007/978-3-031-36357-3_10

open data portals can manifest itself in several ways: Inaccurate information, lack of integrity in official data sets, outdated data or corrupt data sets [3], among others.

To deal with this situation, although there are several approaches that refer to the problem [4], there is no single model integrated with specific metrics to be able to determine which are the most important characteristics that should be incorporated in the implementation of the design for the evaluation of the quality of data published in open data portals. The following articles support the above statement: In the article [3] challenges arise when dealing with quality with open data. In the article [5] it is emphasized that today's organizations do not pay enough attention to the management of the data set. By not publishing quality data, the reuse of data by the citizen is jeopardized [4]. The authors in the article [6] they suggest dimensions that should be used for data quality processes in open data portals. A health data governance strategy with tools is presented in the article [7], additionally complements with concepts and recommendations that will allow countries to generate open data of higher quality, reliable and secure. Finally in the article [8] the risks of quality, integration and authenticity of open data are related.

Data is becoming a business asset for organizations, which is why managing data as an asset is still evolving [9]. For many companies, the starting point in this challenge is to store the greatest amount of data in repositories that facilitate their management; however, the effort to collect and store is wasted if they are not trusted. To guarantee that quality standards are met, an additional effort is required that involves not only the Technology areas but also the business strategy, which defines the importance of the data and the relevant attributes to leverage decision-making. It is at this point where the activities carried out by employees on a day-to-day basis do not allow time to be dedicated to incorporating validations that guarantee the quality of said information. To complement the above,

This document presents the proposal of a model for the evaluation of open data quality where several stages were defined:

E1: Identify the relevant characteristics or dimensions in the quality of open data. For this phase, both a bibliographic review was carried out, as well as the obtaining of opinions from experts on the subject.

E2: Design of the model for the evaluation of open data quality. The selected dimensions are integrated and the calculations for the metrics of the dimensions and the way to obtain the data quality index are defined.

E3: It is validated through a case study.

2 Identification of Dimensions in Data Quality

2.1 Bibliographic Review

Among the bibliographic sources used are IEEE, Springer, Web of Science, Science Direct, MINTIC, Scielo, Scopus, among others. From this bibliographic review whose approach contained the elements of Open Data, Metrics and Data Quality, common themes are identified, thus allowing a group to be proposed which is represented in Fig. 1.

As can be seen in the fig. above, the issue most frequently addressed by the authors is Quality of Data published in Open Data portals. Based on the results of the systematic

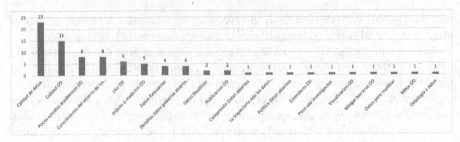

Fig. 1. Common problems in Open Data. Source: Own elaboration

bibliographic review, and once a pre-classification of the types of topics addressed by the articles has been carried out, it is observed that there are some more trends addressed by the authors, of which we can cite some: Academic studies of Open Data [10–15], Open Data Indicators [16–18], Knowledge of the user of open data [19–22], Mitigate Open Data barriers [23], Open Data Path [24].

Although the strategy of publishing Open Data on company portals has made it easier for citizens to have access to information of interest in different areas such as health, education, government, entities, among others; There are several factors that take on importance when publishing the information, such as: Quality of the information, the importance of the data for the citizen, the knowledge of the users of the published information, among other aspects.

As the research space is Data Quality in Open Data portals, one of the activities is to identify the quality dimensions that are most used before publishing in the open data portal. Different authors consider it important to define some dimensions of quality, however, other authors define the same concept, but with different names, which generates ambiguity. Due to the above, it is a priority to identify the articles that discuss the subject, then identify the quality dimensions that have been most addressed in the studies, and those that are considered the most frequent problems in open data portals. Based on the systematic review (Fig. 2).

According to the literature review, the dimensions most referenced by the authors are displayed in Table 1 as shown below.

2.2   Survey

To complement the research, a survey was designed with an Open Data Quality approach applied in a company in the electricity sector, where users among professionals, assistants and technicians who have worked with information could, in the opinion of an expert, issue their preferences or classify according to your experience what would be the most important points to consider when it comes to Quality. This survey identifies the following aspects: Position within the company, Process that supports in the organization, How do you rate the quality of the information that you use in your process for the activities that you develop?, Frequency with which the exercises have been carried out to improve the quality of data you use for your activities, and the dimensions

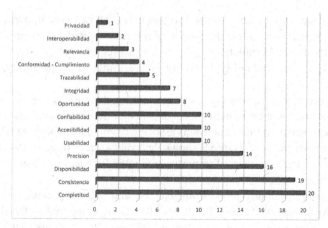

Fig. 2. Dimensions of Quality in Open Data. Source: Own elaboration

Table 1. List of data quality dimensions referenced by authors

DIMENSIONS DATA QUALITY	REFERENCES	TOTAL REFERENCES
Availability	[3–5, 7, 24, 25–35]	16
Completeness	[3–5, 17, 29, 31–34, 36–47]	21
Consistency	[3, 4, 6, 17, 28, 29, 31–33, 36, 37, 40–43, 47–49]	18
Usability	[4–6, 27, 28, 39, 47, 50–52]	10
Opportunity-Present	[4, 6, 28, 31–33, 40, 41, 47, 49]	10
Integrity	[7, 30–32, 43, 49, 50]	7
Accessibility	[5, 6, 27, 33, 34, 40, 42, 49, 50]	9
Reliability	[5, 6, 28, 30, 33, 44, 47, 48, 50]	9
Relevance	[5, 36, 50]	3
Traceability	[4, 28, 44, 47, 49]	5
Interoperability	[6, 27]	2
Precision	[6, 15, 17, 28, 33, 34, 36, 37, 42–44, 47, 53]	13
Present	[28, 33, 47]	3
Conformity-Compliance with standards	[28, 33, 47, 49]	4
Understandability	[28, 33, 47, 54]	4

referenced by the authors are published so that users can rate how important they consider these dimensions to assess the quality of information in the company. The dimensions evaluated were: Completeness, Consistency, Precision, Duplicity, Validity, Relevance, Traceability, Availability, Usability, Accessibility, Interoperability, Reliability, Opportunity.

From this exercise, aspects that are important for the end user are identified, such as: Number of users that make use of the data and their level of importance with respect to the quality dimensions and dimensions associated with data quality that the company should give higher priority. Figure 3 shows the evaluation of dimensions according to expert opinion, where the level of importance is rated for each dimension according to their experience.

Another complementary look at this exercise and that the previous survey throws up, is the satisfaction of the quality of the information compared to the frequency in which quality is applied. It was found that 57.1% of the respondents state that they are moderately satisfied with the quality of the information; however, of this 100% of the population, 50% only applied quality once a year, 41.7% have applied quality 3 times a year, and 8.3% have never applied quality. At this point, the data indicates that little time is spent on data quality, even though the user is moderately satisfied.

On the other hand, regarding users who are very satisfied with the quality of the data, only 25.5% say they have applied quality to their data 3 times a year, another 72.5% do quality to their data at some point and 12.5% have not applied quality to the data.

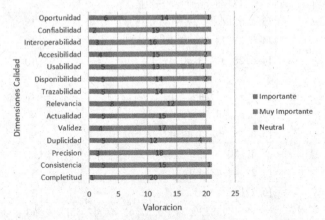

Fig. 3. Qualification Dimensions Employees. Source: Own elaboration

These questions are important in light of this research, since some questions arise such as:

- Is data quality not applied in the company because a methodology to apply is not known?
- Do not have the appropriate tools to apply data quality in the organization?

- Isn't the user responsible for guaranteeing the quality of the data they manage?

Taking into account the above, it is concluded again that since data quality is a relevant issue in organizations, it is an activity that is not very internalized in the processes, for which the scope of this article is very important to leverage this type of needs.

3 Dimensions for the Model

After these exercises, an exploration of the results of the relevance of the quality dimensions was made between the bibliographic review and the results of the surveys applied to the company's experts. Without intending to make a comparison with statistical value, the result can be seen in Fig. 4 where it is evident that some dimensions are more important than others, and dimensions such as Precision, Consistency, Availability, Completeness, Validity are the ones that are at the top of the list. Preferences for these two interest groups.

Given the importance of identifying the most suitable dimensions for the proposed prototype, the following steps are carried out:

- Re-list the dimensions by author depending on the number of articles that reference that dimension.
- Re-enumerate the dimensions by professionals depending on the number of professionals who qualify said dimension.
- The averages given by the previous scores are identified from lowest to highest, thus achieving a prioritization and a final identification of up to 7 dimensions.

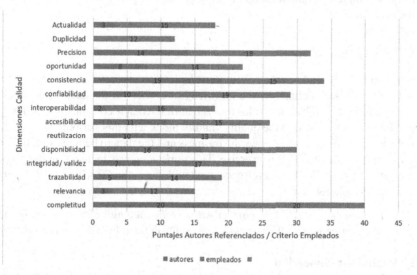

Fig. 4. Association Dimensions Quality Authors/Survey Source: Own Elaboration

Finally, the dimensions Completeness, Accuracy, Reliability, Consistency, Availability, Accessibility, and Integrity/Validity are those that, in a range of 1 to 7, are of greater importance in reference by the authors and in the priority assigned by data professionals on the previously presented slope. It is important to clarify that this project only contemplates the dimensions Completeness, Validity, Availability, and Consistency, it is not ruling out the other dimensions, some are simply defined for analysis and that they will be taken into account to use some of them in the prototype of the Quality Model. Data proposed by this study.

4   Model for Data Quality Evaluation

From the literature review and the dimensions defined in the previous mapping, some metrics referenced by authors and associated with each dimension were identified, which are described below.

4.1   Completeness Dimension

Dimension that allows to control if an attribute defined to work contains its complete or full data. From business experience, data that is complete does not necessarily mean that it is valid, therefore, it is relevant to complement this exercise with the validity dimension of the data to give a more accurate value to the quality index; however, this type of criteria must be defined by the end user who is the owner of the data.

In the proposed Model it is proposed to use the dimension proposed by the author Vetro defined in the article [4] whose formulation corresponds to Percentage of complete cells. The proposal indicates performing the calculation of the percentage of complete cells, this being the formulation that has the greatest impact since the data is reviewed at the attribute level.

4.2   Validity Dimension

Dimension that allows to determine if the values of an attribute are within the ranges, or established values defined by the knowledgeable users of the data. This dimension requires a definition of business rules for each attribute that is considered to be involved, and to be more successful in the quality validity index with this attribute, it is necessary that the functional user, who knows the business and the data to be reviewed, define the rules to be implemented in this exercise. This dimension was included in the proposed model, as a reference for the exercise we work with the author Torchiano [17] where the following formulation applies:

- *pcvc Percentage of cells with correct value (value belonging to the domain) Same.* Percentage of cells with the correct value (value defined by a domain or data range)

4.3   Availability Dimension

Dimension that allows identifying how updated the data is in a period of time. This dimension can be measured by a percentage that reflects whether the data is up to date, in which case its value will correspond to 100% and 0% when the data has lost its validity. Again, this is an additional criterion that the functional user (user who works in a company and is knowledgeable about the business and owner of the data) must consider and will depend on its relevance in the calculation of the quality index.

For the modeling exercise, the formulation presented by the author Vetro is taken as a reference [4] where indicates that said indicator can be analyzed by reviewing Delay in publication.

4.4 Consistency Dimension

This dimension makes it easy for users to determine the number of duplicate records in the data being processed. As the dimension was worked in the Model, it allows the parameterization of a set of attributes where the combination of them facilitates the identification of duplicate records in this parameterization. For the implemented prototype, it is defined that the formulation to work is the one proposed by the author Torchiano [17] whose formulation is the following:

- *Consistency Duplication Number of participant which are duplicated in each lot.* Consistency in the number of components that are duplicated in each batch of data.

4.5 Quality Index

The Quality Index is a fundamental component of the final Model that brings together all the percentage calculations of quality dimensions defined by the end user and gives a result of the quality of the data by applying the metrics of the proposal, based on the final parameterization of the dimensions defined by the user. It is an integrated formula that consolidates the calculation of data quality based on previously defined parameters.

$$IndiceCalidad = \sum_{k=1}^{n} (\% \, Dimensión \, Tabla)$$

n: The number of dimensions involved in the calculation of the Quality Index is defined.

Dimension: It refers to the dimension or dimensions defined by the user in the modeling for the calculation of the quality index.

Finally, with this bibliographic review, it was possible to identify the interest of the community in data quality problems and what are the most applied dimensions and addressed by the authors, this being the point of reference to start the design of the applicable Data Quality Model. For a company in the electricity sector.

5 Validation

For the application of the proposed prototype, open Lightning by Circuit data from a company in the electrical sector published in the MINTIC portal whose data container is "kscf-fk2u" is used.

Once the formulation to be used in each of the dimensions for the proposed model has been defined, an algorithm is implemented at the database level that automatically performs the following processes:

1) Completeness
   a. The variables to be measured in this dimension are defined.

b. The amount of existing data is executed for each parameterized variable vs. the number of total records of the object to be studied

2) Validity
   a. We proceed to define with the end user for each attribute to evaluate the validity rules that must be applied in each attribute
   b. The result of these validations is calculated to identify the % of compliance with this rule.

3) Availability
   a. The validity of the data is calculated as a total of updated days based on the current date vs. the date of the last publication of the data.

4) Consistency
   a. The combination of attributes that must be evaluated where the criterion is non-duplicity in the selection is defined.
   b. Depending on the number of duplicate records, the total consistency percentage is identified vs. the complete data.

5) For each dimension, the percentage of impact on the final result of the index is calculated, data that were previously parameterized to achieve a 100% final rating.

6) The results of each processing or quality calculation are stored in a repository, keeping the quality calculation history and thus a data quality behavior can be arranged over time, facilitating the interpretation and progress over time of the data quality.

Figure 5 presents the behavior of the quality indicator in a period of time (range that the dashboard allows to select in the filter year and structure), which facilitates the visualization of the behavior of the data quality indicator over time. It is evident that the indicator had a problem in its behavior in the month of May since from 94.65% that it had in April it drops to 63.87% for the month of May.

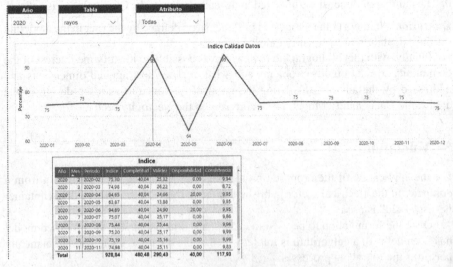

Fig. 5. Lightning Data Quality Index per Circuit Source: Own Elaboration

To understand this behavior, Fig. 6 shows the calculated dimensions and a greater detail of these results, evidencing that the dimensions that had problems during this period were validity and availability, in the department_code attribute where there are 1657 records out of 2142 that did not correspond. to valid data within the range established for the department code. Additionally, in the upper left corner, it is evident that the completeness dimension is the one that provides the most information for the proposed quality index, so the user will be able to apply the necessary controls in a more timely manner to guarantee that this problem does not occur again.

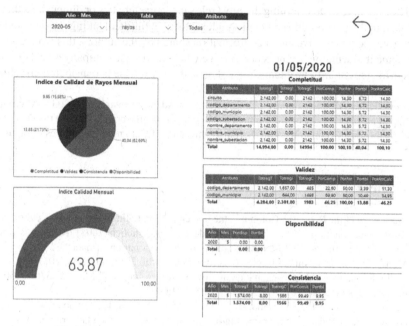

Fig. 6. Detailed index by dimensions Source: Own Elaboration

In addition, the proposal is implemented in a functional prototype that allows obtaining a data quality value, with automatic or semi-automatic calculations.

6 Conclusions

Despite the fact that many works were found around the subject of open data, there is no consensus regarding the relevant dimensions that allow determining the quality of the data; Not all authors publish the metrics associated with the dimensions of data quality that they address in the articles, how to calculate them from open data, and on the other hand, it is found that many authors do not present a definition of an aligned data quality index with the dimensions shown.

This work proposes a Conceptual Model that is specified in a Technological Model through a prototype that allows calculating the Quality Index of Open Data to evaluate its quality, based on the most representative metrics that the systematic review of articles and the criteria from some business users about important dimensions based on business experience.

From the space found in the review of the literature and in the work with experts with a business vision, a contribution is presented in the definition of an Open Data Quality Index composed of metrics that allow calculations of different dimensions related to the data quality, which can be weighted according to the particular conditions of each data source, in addition to allowing the addition of new dimensions if considered, given the modularity of the proposal.

The objective of determining the most relevant characteristics or dimensions that can be linked in the proposed Data Quality Index Model is fulfilled, taking into account that apart from the perspective and the information shared by the authors, this work could be complemented with the business perspective where finally the company on a day-to-day basis evidences quality problems in the data and this exercise is considered enriching.

Acknowledgments. The authors thank the Intelligent Adaptive Environments (GAIA) group for the support and availability of the components used in this degree project. Also to the Department of Informatics and Computing of the National University of Colombia - Manizales Campus.

References

1. Presidency of the Republic. Colombia, the first country in Latin America with a public policy for data exploitation (2018). http://es.presidencia.gov.co/noticia/180417-Colombia-primer-pais-en-Latinoamerica-with-a-public-policy-for-the-exploitation-of-data
2. Mintic. Digital Government Implementation Manual. vol. 2018, pp. 1–38 (2011)
3. Sadiq, S., Indulska, M.: Open data: quality over quantity. Int. J. Inf. Manage. **37**(3), 150–154 (2017). https://doi.org/10.1016/j.ijinfomgt.2017.01.003
4. Vetrò, A., Canova, L., Torchiano, M., Minotas, C.O., Iemma, R., Morando, F.: Open data quality measurement framework: definition and application to Open Government Data. Gov. Info. Q. **33**(2), 325–337 (2016). https://doi.org/10.1016/j.giq.2016.02.001
5. Kubler, S., Robert, J., Neumaier, S., Umbrich, J., Le Traon, Y.: Comparison of metadata quality in open data portals using the Analytic Hierarchy Process. Gov. Info. Q. **35**(1), 13–29 (2018). https://doi.org/10.1016/j.giq.2017.11.003
6. Giovannini, E.: Towards a Quality Framework for Composite Indicators, oecd
7. D'Agostino, M., Marti, M., Mejía, F., de Cosio, G., Faba, G.: Estrategia para la gobernanza de datos abiertos de salud: un cambio de paradigma en los sistemas de información. Revista Panamericana de Salud Pública **41**, 1 (2017). https://doi.org/10.26633/RPSP.2017.27
8. Colborne, A., Smit, M.: Identifying and mitigating risks to the quality of open data in the post-truth era. In: Proceedings - 2017 IEEE International Congress on Big Data, Big Data 2017, vol. 2018-January, pp. 2588–2594 (2018). https://doi.org/10.1109/BigData.2017.8258218
9. Lady International, LADY-DMBOK (2022)
10. Verhulst, S.G., Young, A.: Open Data in Developing Economies: Toward Building an Evidence Base on What Works and How. African Minds (2017). https://doi.org/10.47622/978192833 1599
11. dos Santos, P.X., Guanaes, P.: Open Science, Open Dice: Challenge and Opportunity. Work Education and Health (2018). https://doi.org/10.1590/1981-7746-sol00120

12. Ramírez, A.R., Garro, J.E.: Accountability y sociedad civil: el control político en la era digital. Papel Político **22**(2), 311 (2018). https://doi.org/10.11144/Javeriana.papo22-2.ascc
13. Bonina, C., Scrollini-Ilda, F.: Governing open health data in Latin America
14. Scavuzzo, M., Nitto, E.D., Ardagna, D.: Experiences and challenges in building a data intensive system for data migration. Empir. Softw. Eng. **23**(1), 52–86 (2017). https://doi.org/10.1007/s10664-017-9503-7
15. Oliveira, J., Delgado, C., Assaife, A.C.: A recommendation approach for consuming linked open data. Expert Syst. Appl. **72**, 407–420 (2017). https://doi.org/10.1016/j.eswa.2016.10.037
16. Castillo, H.: María Victoria Martínez M., Hadabell Castillo H., Cristian Grandón G. September, 2018 (2018)
17. Torchiano, M., Vetro, A., Iuliano, F.: Preserving the benefits of open government data by measuring and improving their quality: an empirical study. In: Proceedings - International Computer Software Application Conference, vol. 1, p. 144–153 (2017). https://doi.org/10.1109/COMPSAC.2017.192
18. Pane, J., Paciello, J.: The Cost of Late Payments in Public Procurement. http://standard.open-contracting.org/latest/en/getting_started/contracting_process/
19. Machova, R., Lnenicka, M.: Evaluating the quality of open data portals on the national level. J. Theor. App. Electron. Commer. Res. **12**(1), 21–41 (2017). https://doi.org/10.4067/S0718-18762017000100003
20. Concha, G., Naser, A.: Open data: a new challenge for the governments of the region
21. Danneels, L., Viaene, S., Van den Bergh, J.: Open data platforms: discussing alternative knowledge epistemologies. Gov. Info. Q. **34**(3), 365–378 (2017). https://doi.org/10.1016/j.giq.2017.08.007
22. Ruijer, E., Grimmelikhuijsen, S., Meijer, A.: Open data for democracy: developing a theoretical framework for open data use. Gov. Info. Q. **34**(1), 45–52 (2017). https://doi.org/10.1016/j.giq.2017.01.001
23. Beno, M., Figl, K., Umbrich, J., Polleres, A.: Open data hopes and fears: determining the barriers of open data. In: Proceedings 7th International Conference E-Democracy Open Government CeDEM 2017, pp. 69–81 (2017). https://doi.org/10.1109/CeDEM.2017.22
24. Sieber, R.E., Johnson, P.A.: Civic open data at a crossroads: dominant models and current challenges. Gov. Info. Q. **32**(3), 308–315 (2015). https://doi.org/10.1016/j.giq.2015.05.003
25. Xia, W., Xu, Z., Mao, C.: User-driven filtering and ranking of topical datasets based on overall data quality. In: Proceedings - 2017 14th Web Information System Application WISA Conference 2017, vol. 2018-January, no. 1, pp. 257–262 (2018). https://doi.org/10.1109/WISA.2017.24
26. Zhang, P., Xiong, F., Gao, J., Wang, J.: Data quality in big data processing: Issues, solutions and open problems. In: 2017 IEEE SmartWorld Ubiquitous Intelligence Computing Advanced and Trusted Computed Scalable Computing and Communication Cloud and Big Data Computing. Internet People Smart City Innovations Smart-World/SCALCOM/UIC/ATC/CBDCom/IOP/SCI 2017, pp. 1–7 (2018). https://doi.org/10.1109/UIC-ATC.2017.8397554
27. Dawes, S.S., Vidiasova, L., Parkhimovich, O.: Planning and designing open government data programs: an ecosystem approach. Govern. Inform. Q. **33**(1), 15–27 (2016). https://doi.org/10.1016/j.giq.2016.01.003
28. Safarov, I., Meijer, A., Grimmelikhuijsen, S.: Utilization of open government data: a systematic literature review of types, conditions, effects and users. utr Sch. Gov. **22**(1), 1–24 (2017). https://doi.org/10.3233/IP-160012
29. Abella, A., MOC De-pablos-heredero: Open Data Quality Indicators: The Barcelona Open Data Portal Case Open data quality metrics: Barcelona open data portal case

30. Yoon, S.P., Joo, M.H., Kwon, H.Y.: How to guarantee the right to use PSI in the age of open data: lessons from the data policy of South Korea. Inf. Polity **24**(2), 131–146 (2019). https://doi.org/10.3233/IP-180103

31. Bicevskis, J., Bicevska, Z., Nikiforova, A., Oditis, I.: Data quality evaluation: a comparative analysis of company registers' open data in four European countries. Comput. Sci. Inf. Syst. **17**, 197–204 (2018). https://doi.org/10.15439/2018f92

32. Nikiforova, A.: Open data quality evaluation: a comparative analysis of open data in Latvia. Balt. J. Mod. Comput. **6**(4), 363–386 (2018). https://doi.org/10.22364/bjmc.2018.6.4.04

33. Utamachant, P., Anutariya, C.: An analysis of high-value datasets: a case study of Thailand's open government data. In: Proceeding 2018 15th International Joint Conference on Computer Science and Software Engineering JCSSE 2018, pp. 1–6 (2018). https://doi.org/10.1109/JCSSE.2018.8457350

34. Reiche, K.J., Höfig, E., Schieferdecker, I.K.: Assessment and visualization of metadata quality for government data. In: International Conference on eDemocracy & eGovernment Procedings 21–23 May 2014, CeDEM 2014, Danube University Krems, Austria, pp. 335–346 (2014). http://publica.fraunhofer.de/documents/N-305654.html

35. Ministry of Information and Communication Technologies [MINTIC], MAE. G. GENE . 01 – Master Document, p. 62 (2019), https://www.mintic.gov.co/arquitecturati/630/articles-144764_recurso_pdf.pdf

36. IP 25000, Iso-25012 @ Iso25000.Com, ISO 25000 Software and Data Quality (2021). https://iso25000.com/index.php/en/iso-25000-standards/iso-25012

37. Ahmed, H.H.: Data quality assessment in the integration process of linked open data (LOD). In: Proceedings IEEE/ACS International Conference on Computer Systems and Applications. AICCSA, vol. 2017-Octob, pp. 1–6 (2018). https://doi.org/10.1109/AICCSA.2017.178

38. Kao, C.H., Hsieh, C.H., Chu, Y.F., Kuang, Y.T., Yang, C.K.: Using data visualization technique to detect sensitive information re-identification problem of real open dataset. J. Syst. Archit. **80**(February), 85–91 (2017). https://doi.org/10.1016/j.sysarc.2017.09.009

39. Ruijer, E., Grimmelikhuijsen, S., van den Berg, J., Meijer, A.: Open data work: understanding open data usage from a practice lens. Int. Rev. Adm. Sci. **86**(1), 3–19 (2020). https://doi.org/10.1177/0020852317753068

40. Zhang, R., Indulska, M., Sadiq, S.: Discovering data quality problems: the case of repurposed data. Bus. Inf. Syst. Eng. **61**(5), 575–593 (2019). https://doi.org/10.1007/s12599-019-00608-0

41. Daraio, C., Lenzerini, M., Leporelli, C., Naggar, P., Bonaccorsi, A., Bartolucci, A.: The advantages of an Ontology-Based Data Management approach: openness, interoperability and data quality. Scientometrics **108**(1), 441–455 (2016). https://doi.org/10.1007/s11192-016-1913-6

42. Morbey, G.: Data Quality for Decision Makers (2013)

43. Behkamal, B., Kahani, M., Bagheri, E., Jeremic, Z.: A metrics-driven approach for quality assessment of linked open data. J. Theor. App. Electron. Commer. Res. **9**(2), 64–79 (2014). https://doi.org/10.4067/S0718-18762014000200006

44. Batini, C., Scannapieca, M.: Data-Centric Systems and Applications: Data Quality Concepts, Methodologies and Techniques (2006)

45. Ministry of Information Technology and Communications [MINTIC], fichatecnicacalidad @ tools.datos.gov.co (2019). https://herramientas.datos.gov.co/es/fichatecnicacalidad

46. Icontec, Colombian Technical Standard ISO 55001

47. [fifty] ISO, ISO/IEC 25012 (2021). https://iso25000.com/index.php/en/iso-25000-standards/iso-25012

48. Talukder, M.S., Liang Shen, M., Talukder, F.H., Bao, Y.: Determinants of user acceptance and use of open government data (OGD): an empirical investigation in Bangladesh. Technol. Soc. **56**, 147–156 (2019). https://doi.org/10.1016/j.techsoc.2018.09.013

49. Ferney, M.M.J., Beltran Nicolas Estefan, L., Alexander, V.V.J.: Assessing data quality in open data: a case study. In: 2017 CONIITI 2017 - Conference Proceedings, vol. 2018-January, pp. 1–5 (2018). https://doi.org/10.1109/CONIITI.2017.8273343
50. Ministry of Information and Communication Technologies [MINTIC]. Data Quality Technical Sheet (2019). https://herramientas.datos.gov.co/es/fichatecnicacalidad
51. Zhang, P., Xiong, F., Gao, J., Wang, J.: Data Quality in Big Data Processing: Issues, Solutions and Open Problems
52. Abella, A., Ortiz-De-urbina-criado, M., De-Pablos-heredero, C.: Meloda 5: A metric to assess open data reusability. Prof. la Inf. **28**(6), 8–10 (2019). https://doi.org/10.3145/epi.2019.nov.20
53. Brezočnik, L., Fister, I., Podgorelec, V.: Swarm intelligence algorithms for feature selection: a review. App. Sci. **8**(9), 1521 (2018). https://doi.org/10.3390/app8091521
54. Veljković, N., Bogdanović-Dinić, S., Stoimenov, L.: Benchmarking open government: an open data perspective. Gov. Info. Q. **31**(2), 278–290 (2014). https://doi.org/10.1016/j.giq.2013.10.011

Time Model for the WellProdSim Agent-Based Social Simulator

Jairo E. Serrano[1] (✉) ⓘ, Miguel A. Rivera[2] ⓘ, and Enrique González[2] ⓘ

[1] Universidad Tecnológica de Bolívar, Cartagena, Colombia
jserrano@utb.edu.co
[2] Pontificia Universidad Javeriana, Bogotá, Colombia
{rivera-miguela,egonzal}@javeriana.edu.co

Abstract. This paper focuses on the development of the time control model and its relationship with other agents in the WellProdSim Social Simulator, which assesses the productivity and welfare of peasant families. The simulator adopts an event-driven approach with high concurrency and integrates Belief-Desire-Intention (BDI) reasoning for realistic representation of cognitive processes and decision-making among peasant families. Furthermore, it features a heterogeneous time management system, allowing for diverse time scales and dynamics that account for various time-sensitive factors influencing peasant families' well-being, such as seasonal changes and socio-economic events. Preliminary results demonstrate high-quality simulations, closely resembling real-world scenarios, and provide valuable insights into the lives and challenges faced by peasant families. Additionally, the study identifies areas with potential for improvement, setting the stage for future enhancements and refinements to the simulator. By incorporating event-driven processes, BDI reasoning, and heterogeneous time management, the WellProdSim Social Simulator offers a robust and realistic reading of peasant families' productivity and well-being, with promising prospects for further advancements to improve its effectiveness.

Keywords: Complex-environmental systems · Agent-Based Simulator · Multi-agent systems · Multi-agent simulation

1 Introduction

A large number of peasant families in Colombia do not have adequate technical, organizational and economic capacity to carry out their productive activities [1]. For this reason, there are several initiatives that promote various types of training, support, and delivery of supply to peasants. This provides the opportunity to improve productive capacity and generate greater welfare for the populations that follow this type of program.

Uncertainty about the effectiveness of plans to encourage and promote agricultural improvements among peasants is a latent problem for organizations that promote this type of initiatives. Applying modeling and social simulation tools could mitigate a high degree of uncertainty generated by the particularities of the environment where the plans and assistance to peasants will be implemented.

However, adapting or building a social simulator is not a simple task, so it is beyond the reach of peasants or rural development entities. For this reason, a peasant social simulator was developed - WellProdSim, a tool that is easy to parameterize and adapt to the particularities of Colombian peasants.

With the use of a social simulator, peasant families, their environment, productivity, well-being, and various social phenomena of the world around them can be modeled in each time. By constructing various implementation scenarios, the positive or negative impact of the proposed plans can be measured, and better decisions can be made.

This article will emphasize the implementation of time management in WellProdSim. It will be possible to measure the evolution of productivity and peasant well-being over time. At the same time, being possible to detail the state of plant growth and how it benefits from the interaction and peasant care, achieving a better agricultural product.

This article is composed of seven sections. The first section is this introduction. The second section describes time management in various social simulation tools applied to land use and peasant management, in addition to a state of the art that will provide a general context of the contribution and novelties that will be presented in this paper. The third section will present in more detail the WellProdSim agents and their interaction model. The fourth section will be used to present the requirements presented for the construction of WellProdSim, with an approach from the macro to a detailed view of the micro level of the internal design. In section five, a tour of various generic time management models applicable to WellProdSim is made. The sixth section presents the design and model of time management in WellProdSim, its characteristics and new features implemented. Finally, in section seven, the results of the execution of the simulator based on three prototype scenarios, the positive points and the opportunities for improvement detected are presented.

2 Time Management in Social Simulation Applied to Agriculture

Social simulation becomes relevant as a tool for decision-making support. In this case, specifically to address the problem of achieving the best possible support for field strengthening with scarce resources and very focused investment. There are several approaches to developing social simulators. However, agent-based social simulation was selected for this research, thanks to the versatility, quality of the generated simulator and closeness to real-world modeling that this approach provides. In social simulations converge humans, the main actors of the simulation; the world where they perform their activities; the activity to be simulated; and a time control where interactions are developed.

In the case of human actors, a computational thinking model called BDI, a computational model of reasoning close to human thinking, widely studied in [2], will be applied. And for this work an emotional behavior [3, 4] will be added to the agents, quite useful for modeling the well-being of peasant families in WellProdSim. For the control of the world, hybrid model of cellular automatons will be applied [5, 6]. Since time control is the focus of this work, the following is a review of several examples and state of the art where social simulation is applied, and emphasis is placed on the applied time models.

The selection and application of a time scale according to the needs of the simulation is a constant when developing this type of applications. The work is divided into time units. These time partitions could be fixed, as when traditionally working with cellular automata, applying time steps of the same size. If working with agent-based models they can be dynamic and flexible as used in [7] for the study of the behavior of rodents native to the region when they make changes in land use, giving good results, but still far from an acceptable normalization.

Agent-based social simulation can include several variations on time control. In the case of time control is event-driven [8, 9]. Each action is generated by an agent seeking to finish its work. The actions trigger new events or state updates within the agents. When the simulation reaches the expected result, it ends without the need to be biased to an estimated time or defined steps.

However, most of the related work uses existing tools and frameworks [10]. The vast majority use a step-by-step time advancement model, applying fixed time partitions. This being an opportunity for improvement and focus of this work.

3   WellProdSim Multi-agent Model

In the previous chapter the guidelines and conceptual basis for designing and developing WellProdSim were given. This section will present the interaction model designed for the social simulator, the agents, and their interactions.

Agents are entities that play an active role in the simulator; they have a perception of the world around them. In this case, agents represent various actors in society, including the peasant families, the object of this study. Agents interact with others to accomplish a task. They generate events to transmit information or when they need to deliver, receive, or share a resource. They can be single in the simulation, hundreds, or thousands of them operating concurrently.

The WellProdSim agent model and the goals to be achieved in the simulation will be presented below.

3.1   WellProdSim Agents

To perform the discovery of the main interacting agents in WellProdSim, AOPOA was applied. AOPOA is a methodology used to iteratively design SMAs in a fast and flexible way. As a result, the characterization of six main entities was achieved: the Peasant Families Agent, the World Agent, the Visualizer Agent, the Society Agent, the Perturbation Agent, and the Simulation Manager Agent, as can be seen in Table 1.

Once the agents have been identified, the interactions generated between them will be reviewed in detail in the following section.

3.2   WellProdSim Interactions

WellProdSim is designed to simulate multiple actors in a concurrent manner, and it may be the case that several agents need a single resource, coming into conflict. As a prevention mechanism, it was necessary to design with great precision the operation of the interactions and the events generated by them and thus avoid simulator failures.

Table 1. WellProdSim Agents.

Agents	Goal
Peasant Families	Simulate the actors that affect the productivity and well-being of the peasant family
World	Simulate the actors that affect the productivity and well-being of the peasant family
Society	Simulate the factors that affect the productivity and well-being of the peasant family, including the Market, Banks, Associations, Government and Education
Perturbation	Generate positive or negative perturbations in the other agents
wpsViewer	Display simulation statuses
wpsControl	Build, manage and regulate the simulation

Figure 1 presents the 6 main agents of WellProdSim in a general scheme their interactions. They will be described in more detail below:

- Peasant Family Agent: main agent of the simulation. They perform small-scale agribusiness tasks. They have clearly defined time cycles to interact with the other agents. For example, with *World Agent* they interact by planting the land, maintaining crops, or harvesting; also, with *Society Agent* to buy or sell products and supplies in various ways; with other *Peasant Family Agent* to work collaboratively. Internally it is designed with a human reasoning component called BDI extensively discussed in [2], complemented with emotion management [4], called eBDI.
- World Agent: is the agent that contains and regulates land use by the Peasant Family Agent. This agent provides a terrain and climate model based on real scenarios. The data to build the simulated world were taken from weather stations. As well as the productive cycles were extracted through field work and visits to the region.
- Society Agent: This agent simulates the markets, intermediaries and suppliers where *Peasant Family Agent* acquires supplies or sells its products; it also contains the government, in charge of creating and enforcing the laws and regulations that are the basis of society, including formulating and executing initiatives or generating incentives in favor of the countryside on a recurring basis; the banks are responsible for financial support prior to the planting cycle and subsequent harvesting.
- Perturbation Agent: is the agent in charge of simulating different types of perturbations based on probability models of their occurrence, for example, economic ones that change the purchase or sale price of products, supplies or services; social ones, strikes, significant improvements in education or public order problems; biological ones that can affect crop growth due to pests or improvement depending on the type of fertilizers used; finally, climatic perturbations can generate changes in rain cycles or droughts. The perturbations act positively or negatively the states of the *Society Agent, World Agent,* and *Peasant Family Agent.*

- wpsControl Agent: it builds and controls the simulation life cycle based on an initial parameterization. It is in charge of giving the first virtual time advance that will be replicated by each WellProdSim agent.
- wpsViewer Agent: It is in charge of being the interface to the user to visualize the evolution of the simulation and the effects found in it.

The Table 2. WellProdSim Agent Interactions. Describes in more detail the existing interactions between the Agents, especially those that depend on a time manager to be performed. An interesting point is the inclusion of the emotional BDI model for agents of type *Peasant Family Agent*. With the inclusion of eBDI, the simulated peasant families will not depend exclusively on the cycles established by the time and planting model. They will be able to decide in a better way, including previous knowledge, desires, and emotions to be productive and provide greater well-being for their family. Figure 1 highlights in blue the interactions that are regulated by a time control in WellProdSim.

Table 2. WellProdSim Agent Interactions.

Interaction	Started	Participant	Relation to time
Associating	Peasant Family	Peasant Family	Work Together Organization
Agent Configuration	Simulation Control	All	Initial Timeline
Crop Harvesting	Peasant Family	World	Plant Growth
Simulation starts	Simulation Control	All	Time regulation
Disease check	Peasant Family	All	Plant breeding and sanitation
Crop water supply	Peasant Family	World	Plant Growth
Crop maintenance	Peasant family	World	Crop and weed condition
Climatic perturbation	Perturbation	World	Affecting time
Land preparation	Peasant family	World	Planting time regulated by BDI

For example, when the BDI process activates the interaction "Crop harvesting" within the "Peasant Family agent", an interaction protocol is initiated with the "World agent" to know the state of the crops in a specific instant of virtual time, within the simulation. Time management is important, since plant growth depends on the environment where the plants grow, the water supplied by rainfall according to the season, manual irrigation when necessary and the time elapsed since planting on the land cared for by the simulated peasant families.

Thanks to the rigorous application of the AOPOA methodology, a solid characterization of the agents was achieved and a model of interactions very close to the peasant reality to be simulated is available. This allows for greater precision when calculating productivity and the social impact generated in the peasant families of the region studied.

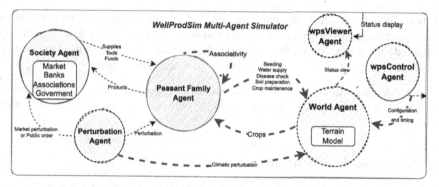

Fig. 1. Time-regulated interactions in WellProdSim.

4 Time Model Requirements

Once the agent model and the interaction model of the multi-agent system have been designed and consolidated, the guidelines for the implementation of the social simulator are established. The following is a set of constraints at a general or macro level and at a detailed or micro level. Based on these restrictions and considering the methodological support, the WellProdSim time management model will be built.

4.1 WellProdSim General Restrictions

To accurately simulate the productivity and well-being of peasant families, it is necessary to model the peasant family and its behavior in detail. Therefore, it is indispensable to mark the constraints in a general way prioritized on the function of time in the simulation, described below:

- Context: the agents depend on it, it regulates the state of mind, the degree of well-being, their environment, the land used for sowing, plant and animal growth, the climate and society with its norms and laws. From the identification of the various agents, cooperative links are created, and interactions are generated to share resources, in this case, land, products, supplies or services. WellProdSim is based on intelligent agents, internally the agents make decisions by applying a reasoning model called emotional BDI. This model prioritizes over time, behavioral norms, opportunities, objectives, and emotions.
- Macro and Micro cycles: the productivity of peasant families is cyclical, closely marked by various micro-level events, such as the family's daily behavior; the productive cycle and the rest cycle; the self-care and well-being cycle; the relationship with peers; and the care of the family. Macro-level events are also considered, such as the sowing or harvesting of crops; the weather; the state of agricultural production; delayed interactions with banks in search of money or other social agents; or being able to solve the most pressing need of the peasant family at the moment of making a decision that impacts their productivity or well-being.
- Heterogeneous times: WellProdSim own design restricts the use of a fixed interval time advance model at a global level. This creates the need for a time management

mechanism that behaves dynamically. The time advance mechanism must be able to integrate the events generated by the various agents involved. In addition, it must transparently allow the internal functioning of the mathematical models used to calculate certain states within the agents and cellular automaton as a whole.

Once the general restrictions of the simulator have been drawn, the necessary implementation features are delimited, which will be described in the following subsection.

4.2 Implementation Constraints in WellProdSim

The desirable characteristics and constraints for the development of the component will be reviewed below:

- Parallelism: parallel execution capability is a must-have feature. The simulation has at least six types of concurrent entities: Peasant Family Agent, World Agent, Perturbation Agent, Society Agent, wpsViewer Agent, and wpsControl Agent. There can be one, hundreds or thousands of concurrently running agents, depending on the parameterization of the running simulation.
- Scalability: is considered from the general design of the simulator. Pseudo-parallelized simulations can usually be run using simple control cycles on a single processing queue. A major problem of serializing a concurrent application is that it becomes hardly scalable and generates a lot of execution bottlenecks. WellProdSim seeks to simulate the real world as accurately as possible, without neglecting the balanced consumption of computational resources.
- Synchronization: In the execution of the distributed simulation, it is possible that the agents are ahead or behind the stipulated global time. WellProdSim must have a synchronization mechanism that provides the highest possible execution performance. Traditional barrier synchronization mechanisms create artificial bottlenecks. With this, they ensure the integrity and consistency of data and agent states. However, WellProdSim detecting a desynchronization of one agent should be resolved with the least possible impact on the states of the other concurrent agents.
- Time control flexibility: the model must allow global time control based on events. The Agents will be in charge of triggering the events according to the required action. However, at the local level, inside the agents or cellular automata, the model must be transparent with step-by-step execution or fixed time intervals of any process that requires it. For example, when it is necessary to calculate mathematical operations or time series runs.
- Efficient use of computing resources: at the moment of receiving events. The creation of a delayed execution should be considered when receiving events that only update the agent's statuses and do not require an instantaneous response. For example, when receiving plant watering or spraying events, the World Agent does not need to update the plant growth status if the Peasant Family Agent has not requested it. This is an important saving in operations and mathematical calculations in the execution of the simulation.

– Event-oriented: agents react to a stimulus, generating events. Event orientation in simulation tends to model the workings of the real world more accurately.

In the following section we will review the types of methods possibly used for time advancement and their application to the model implemented in WellProdSim.

5   Time Models Approaches

For the design of the WellProdSim time control model, the constraints described in the previous section were taken as a basis. It is confirmed that, given the event-driven nature and the heterogeneity of the simulator components in general, it is not possible to apply a single method for time advance.

When developing a simulation, several approaches to time management are possible [11, 12]. One option is to ignore time and consider that there is only a *list of executable events*, only a before and after action performed, a sequence of steps to finish a task. However, due to WellProdSim own design, more control over time management is needed. For example, weather or seasons, agent-generated events and even dates must be able to be described by time units, achieving a complete tracing, and tracking of states in the simulation.

Several timing control options were analyzed. However, three methods used in dynamic simulation models will be taken as a conceptual basis. The methods *"Fixed Incremental Time Advance"* - FITA and *"Next Event Time Advance"* - NETA [13]and Virtual Time were considered the closest to the requirements of WellProdSim.

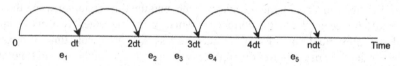

Fig. 2. FITA - Fixed Incremental Time Advance.

In the first method called **FITA** as seen in Fig. 2, time advances in fixed units of duration. Each time delta can be taken as a constant number of seconds, hours or the section of time needed for the simulation. Because of this behavior, agent-generated events may not be synchronized with the overall simulation. However, it can be of great use within the implemented cellular automaton used to predict plant growth and in other mathematical models that need to be computed sequentially.

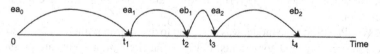

Fig. 3. NETA - Next Event Time Advance.

In the second method called **NETA** related in Fig. 3, the time advance is controlled by the arrival of events (interactions) between the various agents in the simulation. There may be a single general execution queue for the entire simulation, generating or not a possible response or interaction with another required agent.

The single event execution queue model in NETA helps to understand the problem and simplify execution. However, each agent should have its own execution queue to provide better simulation performance. But synchronization problems can occur between the various queues and other inherent elements of parallelism. This feature transforms the implementation into a parallel software development, resulting in the search for another complementary method for its implementation.

The method found, closer to the needs of WellProdSim is called Virtual Time [14–16]. Its authors consider it a paradigm in distributed computing. The implementation was called Time Warp Mechanism. It consists of a synchronization and concurrency control model for simulations running in parallel and/or distributed. Its synchronization mechanism is optimistic, it implements a model where each process is executed as agile as possible and in parallel. In case of a conflict, the desynchronized process performs a backward step to a stable point.

The implementation of Virtual Time is based on the existence of a "global" imaginary clock for the whole simulation. The values returned by the clock will always be positive, and it advances at an indefinite rate with respect to real time. In the implementation, each process (or agent) has a local clock to control the advance of virtual time. In addition, it must exist in a unique space "x", allocated in the virtual world controlled by virtual time "t". So each generated event or action will be considered to occur at a location x and time t – "event(x,t)".

The processes only communicate by exchanging messages when they deem it necessary. Each message is composed of 5 sections, the message itself, the sender's name, an initial virtual time stamp, the receiver's name, and the time stamp of when the message should be received. For the correct operation of the messages, two rules must be considered: the virtual time of sending must be less than the virtual time of receiving and the virtual time of each event in a process must be less than the virtual time of the next event in execution.

In each of the events, a message can be received, the virtual time can be read, the agents' statuses can be updated, or messages can be sent to another agent, triggering new events. In case an event B is generated by an event A, event B cannot start its execution until event A is finished.

6   WellProdSim Time Model

To achieve an optimal WellProdSim timing control model, a rigorous review of the literature in the area was first performed. Applicable conceptual timing control models were selected.

The WellProdSim time model was designed to develop an implementation consistent with the requirements and constraints. In Fig. 4 the simulation agents are visualized all governed by virtual time and internally can vary the models to suit the needs of each agent. The general constraints are covered by applying the following features:

– The simulation must have a universal clock. *WpsControl Agent*, internally will implement a virtual clock and will be in charge of assigning the virtual time at the moment of

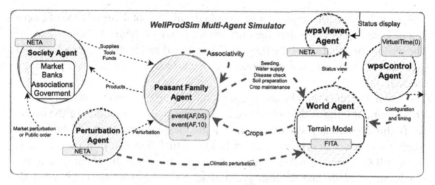

Fig. 4. WellProdSim Time Model.

the creation of the simulation agents. After this point, each agent will use exclusively its local clock.

- Each agent in the simulation will have a local clock, it will be used to mark messages and perform the necessary synchronization operations.
- World model, the virtual local clock of each agent generates delays proportional to the times for the activities being performed by the agent. This generates a harmonic adaptation to the context where the agent lives.
- Each agent has a location in the virtual space. When implemented with BESA [17], the agents have a unique identification in the distributed system.
- Implementation of the agents according to requirements. *Peasant Family Agent* and *wpsControl Agent* are implemented directly with initial global virtual time. *World Agent* implements FITA as time advance mechanism. While *Society Agent*, *Perturbation Agent* and *wpsViewer Agent* are implemented by applying NETA.
- The BESA library will be used as the basis for the development of WellProdSim. Being an event-driven library, the implementation will be transparent and with the expected quality.

The solution to the needs of concurrency, scalability, synchronization, flexibility, resource control and integration with events are presented below:

- Events are generated from agents and are marked by virtual time. In addition, they are based on reactions to emotional BDI decision-making. There is no limit to the number of interactions between agents. Events are asynchronous and are sent to the BESA agent guards. In the case of WellProdSim, an event can be the arrival of the rainy season, triggered by the internal control of the Peasant Family Agent, or a reaction to a query to the World Agent to check the crop status at harvest time.
- The messages will be defined in BESA and there will be a finite and well-defined number of them.
- The content of the message must be defined by a numeric, date, Boolean or Text data type. Each message must be accompanied by the sender's name, receiver's name, an initial virtual timestamp, and a virtual timestamp of when the message is to be received.
- The first rule of virtual time must be complied with: the virtual time of sending must be less than the virtual time of receiving.

- The second virtual time rule must be complied with: the total virtual time of each event in a process must be less than the initial virtual time of the next event in execution.
- The writing or updating of the states will be queued inside the agent and will only be executed when an external agent makes a request that relates the state pending to be updated.
- The reading of states can be done at any time during the simulation.
- The important thing is the coherence in the sequence of execution of the events. To verify this consistency, the timestamps in the messages are used. At the moment of receiving check a desynchronization in the virtual timestamp in the message, the agent will perform a synchronization procedure, returning the agent state to the last synchronized point, and requesting a rollback to the agents that had interacted with that dirty script after that point. The same procedure as in virtual time will be followed.

With the previous statements, the conceptual design of how the implementation of virtual time in WellProdSim should be is marked. One of the advantages in the implementation of the simulator with the BESA libraries. The conceptual design and BESA have very interesting similarities. It can be said that they keep the same line of distributed and transparent design.

7 Results

To evaluate the correct functioning of the weather model, an experiment was constructed using three independent variables, resulting in 27 relevant scenarios. The variables are directly related to the behavior of the peasant families, the climate and the perturbations that can be generated. The Table 3 shows the values used in the independent variables of the experiment.

Table 3. Experimental variables values used to generate 27 different scenarios.

Peasant	Weather	Perturbation
Average	Normal	No Perturbation
Lazy	Wet	Disease
Proactive	Dry	Course

According to the level of attention to the crop, three types of peasant families were considered in the experiment: proactive, average, and lazy. In addition, for climatic conditions, wet, dry, and normal years were defined. Finally, three actions were used for perturbations: a neutral one (i.e., no perturbation); a positive one, when the peasants take a training course to improve their farming skills; and a negative one, when a disease affects the crops.

The validation process focused on the calculation of the biomass generated by a rice crop after 5 months. This variable is considered as the dependent variable measured to evaluate the robustness of the results produced by the time model applied to the

Table 4. Terrain Model Variables for the Experiment.

Configuration Variables	Information Sources
Weather Average Condition	Historical data
Radiation	Historical data
Kind of soils	Government Data
Rainfall	Historical data
Evapotranspiration	FAO
Rice parameters	Government Data

world agent. Approximately five months are simulated, from planting to harvest. The Table 4 shows the configuration variables involved in the definition of the simulation scenarios. Most of the values used for the configuration of these variables are obtained from historical climate information or from official sources such as FAO.

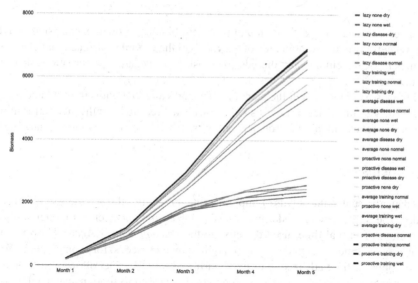

Fig. 5. Expected biomass growth, month by month.

A server with 12 cores and 16 gigabytes of memory was used for the execution of the experiments. Ubuntu Linux 22.04 as operating system, and OpenJDK version 11. Five replicates of the 27 combinations of the independent variables were performed for a total of 135 runs. It took approximately 20 s for each run, simulating 5 months of virtual time. Once each simulation was finished, a file was generated with the data of the behavior of the variables and the results of the estimated biomass for the growth time of the crop.

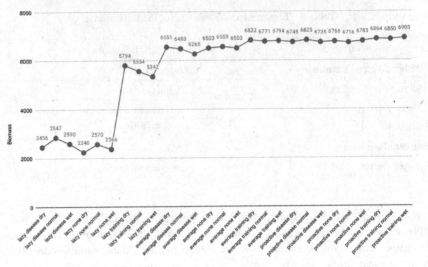

Fig. 6. Comparison of biomass at the fifth month of growth.

As can be seen in Fig. 5 the month-to-month biomass growth is consistent. And it varies according to the combination of the values of the variables assigned for the peasant families tests, the climate and the possible positive or negative perturbations that may occur.

In Fig. 6 a comparison of the plant growth stages after 5 months in simulated time is made. The visualized data are consistent, showing a direct and significant relationship in the normal development of a crop depending on the care applied by the peasant family.

8   Conclusions

This paper presented the details of implementing the WellProdSim social simulator time model. The implemented model integrates a global time management model applying a variation of virtual time, used directly by the *Peasant Family Agent*. However, the agents use the time management model required by their needs, for example, the. *World Agent* applies a time advance with fixed partitions - FITA - that allows it to calculate plant growth on a day-by-day basis. The hybrid approach to time management allows representing the world with greater realism and quality in the generated simulation.

Acknowledgements. The author Jairo Enrique Serrano Castañeda thanks MinCiencias, the Pontificia Universidad Javeriana and the Universidad Tecnológica de Bolívar for the support received to pursue a doctoral degree within *Becas de la Excelencia Doctoral del Bicentenario (corte 1)*.

References

1. Aguilera Diaz, M.: Montes de María: Una subregión de economía campesina y empresarial. Banco de la República, p. 93 (2013)

2. de Silva, L., Meneguzzi, F., Logan, B.: BDI agent architectures: a survey. In: IJCAI International Joint Conference on Artificial Intelligence 2021-January (Line 3), pp. 4914–4921 (2020). https://doi.org/10.24963/ijcai.2020/684
3. Grevenitis, K., Sakellariou, I., Kefalas, P.: Emotional agents make a (bank) run. In: Bassiliades, N., Chalkiadakis, G., de Jonge, D. (eds.) EUMAS/AT-2020. LNCS (LNAI), vol. 12520, pp. 171–187. Springer, Cham (2020). https://doi.org/10.1007/978-3-030-66412-1_12
4. Valencia, D.S., Serrano, J.E., Gonzalez, E.: SIMALL: emotional BDI model for customer simulation in a mall. In: Gonzalez, E., Curiel, M., Moreno, A., Carrillo-Ramos, A., Páez, R., Flórez-Valencia, L. (eds.) CCC 2021. CCIS, vol. 1594, pp. 3–18. Springer, Cham (2022). https://doi.org/10.1007/978-3-031-19951-6_1
5. Fuks, H.: Cellular automata simulations - tools and techniques. In: Modeling Simulation and Optimization - Tolerance and Optimal Control, vol. 1, no. 1 (2010). https://doi.org/10.5772/9044
6. Spicher, A., Fates, N., Simonin, O.: Translating discrete multi-agents systems into cellular automata: application to diffusion-limited aggregation. In: Filipe, J., Fred, A., Sharp, B. (eds.) ICAART 2009. CCIS, vol. 67, pp. 270–282. Springer, Heidelberg (2010). https://doi.org/10.1007/978-3-642-11819-7_21
7. Fur, J., Sall, M.: Using flexible time scale to explore the validity of agent-based models of ecosystem dynamics: application to simulation of a wild rodent population in a changing agricultural landscape. In: Proceedings of 8th International Conference on Simulation and Modeling Methodologies, Technologies and Applications – SIMULTECH, pp. 297–304. SciTePress. (2018). https://doi.org/10.5220/0006912702970304. ISBN 978-989-758-323-0; ISSN 2184-2841
8. Muto, T.J., Bolivar, E.B., González, E.: BDI multi-agent based simulation model for social ecological systems. In: De La Prieta, F., et al. (eds.) PAAMS 2020. CCIS, vol. 1233, pp. 279–288. Springer, Cham (2020). https://doi.org/10.1007/978-3-030-51999-5_23
9. Muto, T.J., Bolivar, E.B., Serrano, J.E., González, E.: Multi-agent CHANS: BDI farmer intentions and decision making. In: Dignum, F., Corchado, J.M., De La Prieta, F. (eds.) PAAMS 2021. LNCS (LNAI), vol. 12946, pp. 151–162. Springer, Cham (2021). https://doi.org/10.1007/978-3-030-85739-4_13
10. Abar, S., Theodoropoulos, G.K., Lemarinier, P., O'Hare, G.M.: Agent based modelling and simulation tools: a review of the state-of-art software. Comput. Sci. Rev. **24**, 13–33 (2017). https://doi.org/10.1016/J.COSREV.2017.03.001
11. Ferro, R., Cordeiro, G.A., Ordonez, R.E.C.: Dynamic modeling of discrete event simulation. In: Proceedings of the 10th International Conference on Computer Modeling and Simulation - ICCMS 2018 (2018). https://doi.org/10.1145/3177457
12. Chen, S., Hanai, M., Hua, Z., Tziritas, N., Theodoropoulos, G.: Efficient direct agent interaction in optimistic distributed multi-agent-system simulations. In: SIGSIM-PADS 2020 - Proceedings of the 2020 ACM SIGSIM Conference on Principles of Advanced Discrete Simulation, pp. 123–128. ACM, New York (2020). https://doi.org/10.1145/3384441.3395977
13. Law, A.M.: Simulation Modeling and Analysis, 5th edn (2015)
14. Jefferson, D.R.: Virtual Time. Technical report (1985)
15. Jefferson, D.R., Barnes, P.D.: Virtual time III: unification of conservative and optimistic synchronization in parallel discrete event simulation. In: 2017 Winter Simulation Conference (WSC), Las Vegas, NV, USA, pp. 786–797 (2017). https://doi.org/10.1109/WSC.2017.8247832
16. Fujimoto, R.M., et al.: Parallel discrete event simulation: the making of a field. In: 2017 Winter Simulation Conference (WSC), Las Vegas, NV, USA, pp. 262–291 (2017). https://doi.org/10.1109/WSC.2017.8247793
17. González, E., Bustacara Medina, C., Avila, J.: Agents for concurrent programming. In: Communicating Process Architectures, vol. 61, pp. 157–166. IOS Press (2003)

World Model for the WellProdSim Agent-Based Social Simulator

Miguel A. Rivera[1] (iD), Jairo E. Serrano[2](✉) (iD), and Enrique González[1] (iD)

[1] Pontificia Universidad Javeriana, Bogotá, Colombia
{rivera-miguela,egonzal}@javeriana.edu.co
[2] Universidad Tecnológica de Bolívar, Cartagena, Colombia
jserrano@utb.edu.co

Abstract. This paper presents the design, implementation, and testing of the WellProdSim world model, a comprehensive social simulator tailored for analyzing peasant families' productivity and social well-being. It encompasses a land control module that facilitates crop growth simulation and accounts for social phenomena such as communication and cooperation within the social and productive context. Additionally, the simulator integrates geographical characteristics and climatic conditions of the region to ensure accurate representation of the environment. Plans are underway to incorporate a BDI (Belief-Desire-Intention) emotional agent module into the world model, which will represent peasants and other social actors, enhancing the simulator's realism in portraying human decision-making processes. The world model has demonstrated success in 27 initial scenarios, utilizing real data from the Montes de Maria region in Colombia, thereby validating its effectiveness in capturing real-world conditions. By focusing on crucial elements such as land control, regional characteristics, and climatic conditions, the WellProdSim world model offers a valuable tool for understanding and addressing the unique challenges faced by peasant families.

Keywords: Complex-environmental systems · Agent-Based Simulator · Multi-agent systems · Multi-agent simulation

1 Introduction

A This paper will address the design of the terrain and the world used in WellProdSim. The focus of the simulator is peasant families, and an appropriate definition will first be agreed upon. A peasant family could be defined as "*a basic multifunctional unit of social organization, crop cultivation, and general animal husbandry as the primary means of livelihood. The family coexists around a specific traditional culture closely linked to the way of life of small rural communities* [1]". Once the concept of the peasant family has been defined, to facilitate its study in the productive and well-being areas, the peasant family will be modeled as a unit, not as independent members. Finally, it is essential to understand the social fabric surrounding families, understanding the social fabric as the implicit norms, customs, and culture that builds ties and interactions that lead peasant families to seek the same common goal closely linked to the region where they develop [2].

© The Author(s), under exclusive license to Springer Nature Switzerland AG 2023
V. Agredo-Delgado et al. (Eds.): CCC 2022, CCIS 1775, pp. 150–163, 2023.
https://doi.org/10.1007/978-3-031-36357-3_12

The design and development of social simulators can be considered from different approaches. In this case, the approach used for the social simulation is based on multi-agent systems, due to its versatility and closeness to represent the entities and their interactions as they occur in the real world and, based on previous successful experiences around social simulation [3, 4]. In this case, the agents represent the actors of the simulation (peasants, lands, etc.), the interactions produced among them, having a behavior close to reality.

In this version of WellProdSim the overall emphasis is on small-scale agro-industrial production by peasant families. It is essential to model the emerging behaviors related to land use, for example, crop growth resulting from planting and harvesting of various types of plants; the reaction to the behavior of the climate and seasons of the region; pests or diseases; and the positive or negative impact resulting from peasant intervention. To model correctly and close to reality, the geographical area of Montes de Maria -MM- was taken as a case study [5]. In MM there is a reliable sample of all the phenomena to be studied by applying WellProdSim. On the other hand, the study of the well-being of peasant families will be analyzed in a different article, given the complexity that needs to be addressed.

This article is composed of six sections. After the introduction. The Sect. 2 discusses the management of a virtual world in a social simulator with applications to agriculture in general, including a conceptual framework on space models and their applicability. The Sect. 3 describes the model of the simulation's base multi-agent system and its interactions. The Sect. 4 emphasizes the requirements and constraints of the world model. Additionally, the design of the world is explained, starting from a macro point of view, up to a detailed one. Section 5 describes the experiments and tests, with their respective results. Finally, Sect. 6 presents the conclusions and future work of this social simulator.

2 Virtual World Management in Social Simulation Applied to Agriculture

Peasant families must make the land produce according to the conditions that are developing; they take advantage of every opportunity available to them to maximize their production and improve their well-being; they can also be affected by multiple social, economic, and public order phenomena in their region. Peasant families interact with various types of organizations, in some cases to purchase products or services, to offer their production, or to seek technical or economic assistance or improvements in their general well-being. The implementation and use of WellProdSim, will allow the study of these phenomena and provide a holistic and consistent decision-making from the simulated environment.

With the proper use of a social simulator, phenomena related to the productivity and well-being of peasant families could be modeled with high accuracy. However, it is necessary to select the appropriate spatial models to simulate the terrain where peasant families interact in WellProdSim. Among the general modeling requirements is the need to describe the geographic characteristics of the region, the climatic conditions, the crop growth, and the constitution of the social fabric of the region. The four most common types of spatial representations used for terrain representation are described below:

- Continuous space: represents abstract (non-geographic) spaces where agents move or interact without constraints. Their focus is on spatial interaction, statistical relationships, and queueing [6]. They have applications in housing search and/or selection, as well as in pedestrian simulations.
- Geographic space: like the continuous space model, with the addition of an explicit reference to geographic locations, using a coordinate [7]. An interesting aspect of this model is the implementation of states and features attached to a geographic point, providing an extremely useful context. It can be used to represent product transportation, peasant mobility, and various law and order effects.
- Cellular Space: its representation is based on a grid, which in turn, can represent a continuous or geographic space. It is used in many applications. For example, to model the growth at different scales of vegetation [8], the movement of crowds [9], in wayfinding [10] or the description of social dynamics [11, 12].
- Topological Space: composed of a graph where objects (agents) are connected by vertices (routes) representing the neighborhood interaction. The network describes the routes and determines which agents can interact. This approach is useful for modeling the neighborhood between plots of land [13], belonging to different peasant families.

Once the different types of existing terrain models were analyzed, a hybrid world control model was designed and implemented in the social simulator, explained in the Sect. 3.

The model of the multi-agent system used in WellProdSim will be described below. The integration with the various types of actors interacting in the simulation and the application of the spatial models according to the desired applicability in the social simulator.

3   WellProdSim Multi-agent System Model

WellProdSim was designed to achieve a better understanding of social and productive dynamics in complex environments; specifically, a multi-agent system - MAS - was conceived. Figure 1 presents the high-level agent-world interaction model.

In this case, agro-industrial productivity is evaluated in terms of maximizing the growth of the biomass of the vegetation layer. The biomass represents the result of the cultivation of various products native to the region, such as rice and yams. Actions taken by the peasant families, such as irrigation and fertilization of crops, and of course their agricultural skills, increase or decrease productivity levels. In addition, the environmental and meteorological conditions of the region positively or negatively affect the cultivation of the crops.

Using WellProdSim it is possible to study the dynamics and emerging behavior patterns of the agents representing the peasant families in the region. By means of micro-scale simulation, family members and plant growth can be studied. At the macro-scale, the social fabric and market behavior can be analyzed. Thus, achieving a better

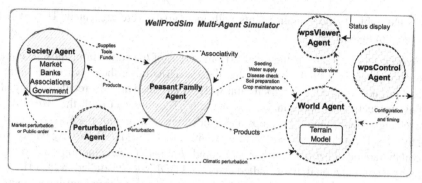

Fig. 1. WellProdSim MAS Model. (Interactions)

understanding of the effects of policies and their positive or negative impact on peasant agriculture. This allows for better decision-making on where to focus resources and technical support from organizations that promote good practices and improvements in productivity and social well-being of peasant families.

3.1 WellProdSim Agents

The macro agents of WellProdSim will be introduced in the following. The terrain model is a fundamental part of the *World Agent* in WellProdSim. The agents of type *Peasant Family Agent* interact continuously and concurrently with *World Agent* to obtain information of the terrain state or plant growth. However, the interaction can be two-way, changing the states of the *World Agent* and affecting the growth of crops and topsoil. It should also be noted that *Perturbation Agent* can also generate extreme variant conditions, such as heavy rains, which modify the behavior of the entities included in the terrain model in general.

Table 1. WellProdSim Agents.

Agents	Goal
Peasant Families	Simulate the actors that affect the productivity and well-being of the peasant family
World	Simulate the actors that affect the productivity and well-being of the peasant family
Society	Simulate the factors that affect the productivity and well-being of the peasant family, including the Market, Banks, Associations, Government and Education
Perturbation	Generate positive or negative perturbations in the other agents
wpsViewer	Visualize simulation states
wpsControl	Create, manage, and regulate the simulation

In the Table 1, the 6 main agents with their goals were presented. They will be described in more detail below:

- *Peasant Family Agent:* is the main axis and focus of the simulation study. The main economic activity of the peasant families is agriculture; they own small animals and sell the fruits of their agricultural work to intermediaries or retailers. They also buy products and inputs in various markets. They interact with the *World Agent* exchanging information on crops and productivity; also, with the *Society Agent* to buy or sell products and supplies; and with other *Peasant Family Agent* to work collaboratively. *Peasant Family Agent* could simulate human emotions and thinking using a computational model called emotional BDI, widely studied in [3, 14].
- *World Agent:* designed to simulate the behavior of the environment where peasant families develop. The *World Agent* has a terrain and climate model based on real data and scenarios. The data to build the simulated world are taken from weather stations, maps of the region and field work directly with the peasant families. The specific composition and design of this agent will be discussed in the Sect. 4.
- *Society Agent:* it is considered as the third actor in the simulation. At this point, the *Society Agent* internally simulates the markets in which the production generated by the *Peasant Family Agent* is offered; the intermediaries, in charge of being the bridge between the peasant families and the markets; the suppliers, who have the necessary supplies to grow the crops; the government, in charge of creating and enforcing the laws and basic norms of the society, in addition to formulating and executing initiatives and incentives in favor of the field; the banks provide initial financial support for the sowing. Some non-profit organizations are also considered as part of the Society Agent. Its implementation is based on reactive agents, endowed with behaviors based on the probability of occurrence of an action at the request of the *Peasant Family Agent*.
- *Perturbation Agent:* there are several types of perturbations, such as economic ones that change the purchase or sale price of products, supplies, or services; social ones, strikes, significant improvements in education or public order problems; biological ones that can affect the growth of crops due to pests; finally, climatic perturbations can generate changes in rain cycles or droughts. The perturbations act positively or negatively the states of the *Society Agent, World Agent,* and *Peasant Family Agent*. They will be implemented as agents controlled by a probability model that generates the perturbations based on real data from the environment.
- *wpsControl Agent:* this agent is responsible for configuring the simulation according to the initial parameterization and modeling of the *Society Agent, World Agent, Peasant Family Agent,* and other variables associated with productivity and peasant well-being. These agents will be implemented as reactive agents, responding to the reception of simulation control commands from external input stimuli.
- *wpsViewer Agent:* in charge of being the user interface to visualize the evolution of the simulation and the effects found in it. It will be implemented as a hybrid reactive agent and an observer pattern of the simulation.

WellProdSim being a multi-agent system, agents interact and/or cooperate to achieve a specific task to perform to satisfaction, for example, to generate as many crops as possible. Interactions emerge when it is required to share information or resources,

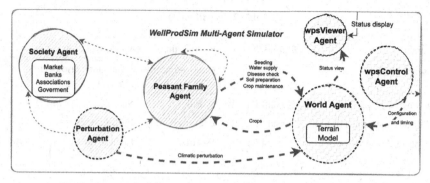

Fig. 2. WellProdSim, with highlighted interactions of World Agent

which are usually finite, and their access is controlled. The following will emphasize how these interactions occur and the protocols that are activated occur.

3.2 WellProdSim Interactions

WellProdSim is designed to simulate multiple agents concurrently, as shown in Fig. 2. The figure highlights the interactions relevant to the *World Agent*. In such a simulation, it may be the case that several agents need a single resource, coming into conflict. As a prevention mechanism, it was necessary to design the operation of the interactions and the events generated by them, and thus avoid simulator failures.

Table 2. Interactions Between WellProdSim Agents.

Interaction	Started	Participant	World Relation
Agent configuration	wpsControl	World	Automatons
Get information	Peasant Family	World	Receive information
Start the simulation	wpsControl	Simulation	Start the simulation
Crop maintenance	Peasant Family	World	Crop maintenance, in this case modify default values of the terrain
Climate Perturbation	Perturbation	World	When a climatic perturbation occurs
Land Preparation	Peasant Family	World	World & prior to the start of the planting season, cleaning the land and resetting land variables
Crop Harvesting	Peasant Family	World	Crop harvesting

(*continued*)

Table 2. (*continued*)

Interaction	Started	Participant	World Relation
Disease check	World	Peasant Family	When a disease occurs, report it
Seeding of crops	Peasant Family	World	Start of crop planting cycle
Requesting supplies or tools	Peasant Family	Peasant Family	Fulfill needs
Supplying water to crops	Peasant Family	World	Plant growth

The Table 2 describes in more detail the existing interactions between the Agents, especially those that depend on a time manager to be performed. An interesting point is the inclusion of the BDI model for agents of type *Peasant Family*. The use of BDI in agents means that in a planting interaction, for example, they not only depend on the world model and the time to know when to sow. It also implies the reasoning of the *Peasant Family Agent* itself for the availability of various supplies, resources, and tools to be productive.

4   WellProdSim World Model

In the previous section the multi-agent system representing WellProdSim was presented. Next, the requirements and constraints of the model for the implementation of the social simulator are highlighted. In addition, the hybrid terrain model designed for WellProdSim will be presented in more detail.

4.1   World Model Requirements

In the design process of the social simulator, six relevant requirements were identified with the implementation of the world model:

- *Spatial location*: locate the farms and the peasant who own them.
- *Land use*: simulate different land uses within the farm.
- *Based on real data*: characterize the specific geographical features of the studied region.
- *Simulate vegetation growth*: to estimate the growth of the crop cover within the plot.
- *Flexible communication patterns*: support diverse communication patterns present in rural agricultural societies.
- *Integration with MAS*: seamlessly integrate with the developed multi-agent system.

The above requirements were taken as the basis for the design of the layers and each of their functionalities.

In this case, the development of the world model required different types of terrain models (see Fig. 3) according to the need of each simulated element [15]. A hybrid model was designed that includes three types of space models and is organized in layers. Each of the layers uses a different type of automaton and covers a specific need of the

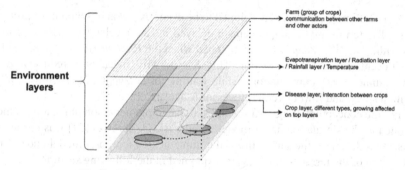

Fig. 3. Time-regulated interactions in WellProdSim.

model. For example, a cellular space model [16] represents land use and supports the simulation of vegetation growth, with each cell of the automaton being the size of a farm, belonging to a peasant family; a topological model [17] includes communication and transportation phenomena; and a geographic model [18] is used for data related to land ownership, land use planning and road layout. This combination of models allows for accurate representation of social, production and meteorological phenomena, as well as the reality of the simulated environment. The convergence of these spatial models makes it possible to more faithfully capture the reality to which the actors in the simulation are exposed.

In the first stage of development, the most relevant point for the terrain model was the implementation of the estimation of crop growth. From the historical climatic information (radiation, precipitation, and temperature), the evapotranspiration -EV-. This key variable is calculated by applying the FAO-56 method [19] and the CROPWAT tool [20]. EV is a variable that describes the evaporation of water from the plant surface and is closely related to plant growth, represented as biomass.

Biomass is directly related to crop growth as a function of EV. Good soil management and care by the peasant family generates a lower loss of EV in crops and an increase in agricultural production. On the other hand, adverse weather conditions generate a greater loss of EV in crops and a decrease in agricultural production.

In fact, other factors may influence plant growth or the development of life in general on the land; for example, salinity, soil fertility, fertilizer use or withholding, lack of disease and/or pest control must be considered. In the proposed approach, these factors affect the value of EV, which is the main variable needed for the calculation of crop biomass.

In the calculation of biomass at a given time of crop growth, a distinction is made between the reference EV of the crop ET_0, one under standard conditions and one under non-standard conditions. ET_0 is a parameter that expresses the EV power of the atmosphere. Good management of the above parameters leads to healthy crop production. However, due to low crop maintenance, such as plant diseases, or environmental constraints. Reduction in crop growth usually occurs when the value of EV decreases. In the opposite case, VS increases when good crop management and maintenance, organic fertilizers or manures are used, and when weather conditions or plant irrigation are favorable.

WellProdSim, by design, is developed to be event-driven and run on multiprocessor servers. The terrain model implements a delayed update mechanism. The state of the crops within the *World Agent* is only updated when the *Peasant Family Agent* sends an explicit event requesting information. This delayed write mechanism reduces the time spent on unnecessary computations while waiting for an agent call. Therefore, higher execution speed and lower overall processor usage are obtained.

Once the conceptual design was completed, the implementation of the terrain model integrated to the simulation agent model and the BESA libraries [21] was carried out. This section describes the interactions, the implemented temporal model and the final construction of the terrain model layers, explained in the following section.

4.2 Crop Layer Interactions

The interaction between the different layers, each representing a variable used to calculate crop growth, is shown in Fig. 4. These variables constitute the core of the *World Agent*. As can be seen, the crop layer depends on the evapotranspiration, solar radiation, precipitation, and temperature layers.

The *Peasant Family Agent* can interact directly with the disease layer to query the status of the crop, and to modify the health conditions of the crop; for example, to cure the plants or treat them. And, at any time, the peasant can interact with the crop layer to modify the growing conditions, for example, for planting, watering, or fertilizing, and for the extraction of agricultural production.

For the calculation of the internal values of the layers, the variables described in FAO56 were used, derived from the Penman-Monteith equation [22]. A brief description of each layer is included in the following paragraphs.

- *Short wave radiation layer:* this layer results from the balance between incoming radiation from the sun and reflected radiation from the earth. The values of this layer are taken from historical values obtained from open databases.
- *Rainfall layer:* this layer reproduces the probability of rainfall on a given date, based on historical values obtained from open databases.
- *Temperature layer:* this layer provides information on the average daily temperature on a given date from a predictive model trained with real data.
- *ET_0 layer:* this layer represents the amount of water returned to the atmosphere, based on evaporation and plant transpiration. This layer is calculated from the meteorological values of the study region. The key update equation is $ET_c = ET_0 * K_c$, where the coefficient K_c depends on the type of crop being simulated, defining favorable or unfavorable conditions for plant growth.
- *Disease layer:* is the layer that represents the probability of a crop getting sick or being attacked by a pest; thus, it is used to model the drop in productivity and put the peasant's food security at risk.
- *Crop layer:* this layer represents and models the growth of the different types of crops grown in the region; common crops are cassava, yams, corn, rice and other tropical products.

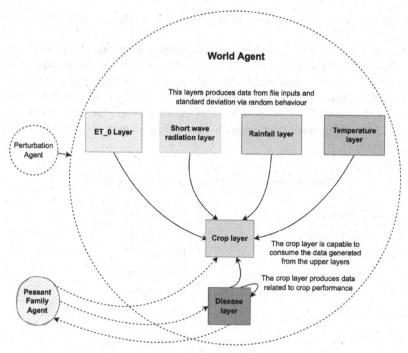

Fig. 4. Environment layers interactions.

5 Results

An experiment with three independent variables was designed to evaluate the correct functioning of the world model, resulting in 27 relevant scenarios. Each scenario was configured by assigning different values to variables related to the behavior of peasant families, climatic conditions, and the occurrence of perturbations. The Table 3 shows the values used for the independent variables of the experiment.

Table 3. Experimental variables values used to generate 27 different scenarios.

Peasant	Weather	Perturbation
Average	Normal	No Perturbation
Lazy	Wet	Disease
Proactive	Dry	Course

According to the level of attention to the crop, three types of peasant families were considered in the experiment: proactive, average, and lazy. In addition, for climatic conditions, wet, dry, and average years were defined. Finally, three actions were used for perturbations: a neutral one (i.e., no perturbation); a positive one, when peasants take a training course to improve their farming skills; and a negative one, when a disease affects crops.

The validation process focused on the calculation of the biomass generated by a rice crop. This variable is considered as the dependent variable measured to evaluate the robustness of the results produced by the field model. Approximately five months are simulated, from sowing to harvest. Table 4 shows the configuration variables involved in defining the simulation scenarios. Most of the values used for the configuration of these variables are obtained from historical climate information or from official sources such as FAO.

Table 4. Terrain Model Variables for the Experiment.

Configuration Variables	Information Sources
Weather Average Condition	Historical data
Radiation	Historical data
Kind of soils	Government Data
Rainfall	Historical data
Evapotranspiration	FAO
Rice parameters	Government Data

For the execution of the experiments, a server with 12 cores and 16 gigabytes of memory was configured. The operating system used was Ubuntu Linux in its latest version, 22.04, and Java version 11. Five replications of the 27 combinations of the experiment's independent variables were performed for a total of 135 runs. It took approximately 20 s for each run. Once each simulation was finished, a file was generated with the data on the behavior of the variables and the results of the estimated biomass for the growth time of the crop.

As can be seen in Fig. 5, the experimental results show a coherent agricultural production in the expected behavior according to the type of peasant in its three variants: lazy, average, and proactive. Being the lazy type of peasant the one that has the worst performance with their crops due to the lack of attention to the care and maintenance of the land.

Figure 6 shows how the behavior in the face of the perturbations was as expected. Formation being a positive perturbation, an increase in agro-industrial production was observed. On the other hand, diseases decreased the expected agricultural production. It can be observed that being an average peasant, he takes care of his crops and there are no major production losses.

6 Conclusions

This paper presented the details of the implementation of a world model for a social simulator. Thanks to this implementation, the WellProdSim social simulator managed to incorporate a combination of spatial models such as continuous space, geographic

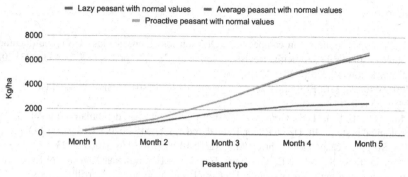

Fig. 5. Expected agro-industrial production by type of peasant.

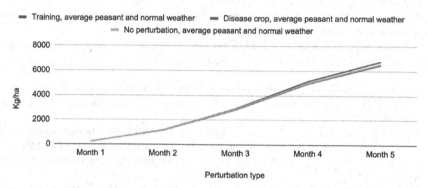

Fig. 6. Effect of perturbations on agro-industrial production.

space, cellular space, and topological space in a layered manner. This hybrid approach allows to capture the reality of the relationships more faithfully between simulation entities: peasant actions, terrain and crops, evapotranspiration, radiation, precipitation, temperature, and crop diseases.

In addition, the terrain model can make use of real climatic and geographic data to predict more detailed scenarios. Applying modulation of the variables involved in the evapotranspiration calculation allows considering positive and negative influences related to crop growth.

The results obtained in the 27 scenarios built according to the types of peasants, climate behavior and diseases interacting with the world, demonstrate the soundness of this approach as a support in the decision making of the social simulator.

Acknowledgements. The author Jairo Enrique Serrano Castañeda thanks MinCiencias, the Pontificia Universidad Javeriana and the Universidad Tecnológica de Bolívar for the support received to pursue a doctoral degree within *Becas de la Excelencia Doctoral del Bicentenario (corte 1)*.

References

1. Edelman, M.: ¿Qué es un campesino? ¿Qué son los campesinados? Un breve documento sobre cuestiones de definición. Revista Colombiana de Antropología **58**(1), 153–173 (2022). https://doi.org/10.22380/2539472X.2130
2. Tellez Murcia, E.I.: El sentido del tejido social en la construcción de comunidad. Polisemia **10**, 9–23 (2010)
3. Muto, T.J., Bolivar, E.B., González, E.: BDI multi-agent based simulation model for social ecological systems. In: De La Prieta, F., et al. (eds.) PAAMS 2020. CCIS, vol. 1233, pp. 279–288. Springer, Cham (2020). https://doi.org/10.1007/978-3-030-51999-5_23
4. Valencia, D.S., Serrano, J.E., Gonzalez, E.: SIMALL: emotional BDI model for customer simulation in a mall. In: Gonzalez, E., Curiel, M., Moreno, A., Carrillo-Ramos, A., Páez, R., Flórez-Valencia, L. (eds.) CCC 2021. CCIS, vol. 1594, pp. 3–18. Springer, Cham (2022). https://doi.org/10.1007/978-3-031-19951-6_1
5. Aguilera Diaz, M.: Montes de María: Una subregión de economía campesina y empresarial. Banco de la República, p. 93 (2013)
6. Torrens, P.M.: Proceedings of the IEEE/WIC/ACM International Conference on Intelligent Agent Technology, IAT 2007, Institute of Electrical and Electronics Engineers Inc., pp. 63–66 (2007)
7. Benenson, I.: Modeling population dynamics in the city: from a regional to a multi-agent approach. Discrete Dyn. Nat. Soc. **3**(2–3), 149–170 (1999). https://doi.org/10.1155/S10260 22699000187
8. Muto, T.J., Bolivar, E.B., González, E.: Multi-agent CHANS: BDI farmer intentions and decision making. In: Dignum, F., Corchado, J.M., De La Prieta, F. (eds.) PAAMS 2021. LNCS, vol. 12946, pp. 151–162. Springer, Cham (2020). https://doi.org/10.1007/978-3-030-85739-4_13
9. Hughes, R.L.: The flow of human crowds. Ann. Rev. Fluid Mech. **35**, 169–182 (2003). https://doi.org/10.1146/ANNUREV.FLUID.35.101101.161136
10. Sud, A., Andersen, E., Curtis, S., Lin, M.C., Manocha, D.: Real-time path planning in dynamic virtual environments using multiagent navigation graphs. IEEE Trans. Vis. Comput. Graph. **14**(3), 526–538 (2008). https://doi.org/10.1109/TVCG.2008.27
11. Sakoda, J.M.: The checkerboard model of social interaction. J. Math. Sociol. **1**(1), 119–132 (2010). https://doi.org/10.1080/0022250X.1971.9989791
12. Schelling, T.C.: Dynamic models of segregation. https://doi.org/10.1080/0022250X.1971.998 9794
13. Crooks, A., Heppenstall, A., Malleson, N.: Agent-based modeling. In: Comprehensive Geographic Information Systems, vol. 3, pp. 218–243. Elsevier (2017). https://doi.org/10.1016/B978-0-12-409548-9.09704-9
14. de Silva, L., Meneguzzi, F., Logan, B.: BDI agent architectures: a survey. In: IJCAI International Joint Conference on Artificial Intelligence 2021-January (Line 3), pp. 4914–4921 (2020). https://doi.org/10.24963/ijcai.2020/684
15. Wainwright, J., Mulligan, M.: Environmental Modelling: Finding Simplicity in Complexity, 2nd edn, pp. 1–475 (2013). https://doi.org/10.1002/9781118351475
16. Li, W.: Nonlocal cellular automata. In: Pattern Formation in the Physical and Biological Sciences, pp. 189–200 (2018). https://doi.org/10.1201/9780429493362-10
17. Crooks, A., Castle, C., Batty, M.: Key Challenges in Agent-Based Modelling for Geo-Spatial Simulation. Technical report (2008)
18. Crooks, A.A.T., Malleson, N., Manley, E.E.J., Heppenstall, A.J.: Agent-based modelling and geographical information systems: a practical primer, p. 378 (2018)

19. Zotarelli, L., Dukes, M.D., Romero, C.C., Migliaccio, K.W., Morgan, K.T.: Step by Step Calculation of the Penman-Monteith Evapotranspiration (FAO-56 Method). Doc. AE459, University of Florida (2010). https://edis.ifas.ufl.edu/pdffiles/AE/AE45900.pdf
20. Land & Water — Food and Agriculture Organization of the United Nations (2022)
21. González, E., Bustacara Medina, C., Avila, J.: Agents for concurrent programming. In: Communicating Process Architectures, vol. 61, pp. 157–166. IOS Press (2003)
22. Pereira, L.S., Allen, R.G., Smith, M., Raes, D.: Crop evapotranspiration estimation with FAO56: past and future. Agric. Water Manag. **147**, 4–20 (2015). https://doi.org/10.1016/j.agwat.2014.07.031

Author Index

V. Agredo-Delgado et al. (Eds.): CCC 2022, CCIS 1775, p. 165, 2023.
https://doi.org/10.1007/978-3-031-36357-3

Printed in the United States
by Baker & Taylor Publisher Services